Fat Burner

Super Fuel:

The easy way to melt off pounds

Fat Burners

We have to eat in order to lose weight. This simple truth always elicits a certain amount of skepticism. It's deeply engraved in our minds that we must avoid calories, refuse fatty foods, and banish evil carbohydrates! And it's because so many of us believe this that so many people in this country are overweight. But whether we follow the latest diet in Hollywood or the one practiced at the office, nothing works in the long run. The bitter result is the "yo-yo effect." We've struggled tediously to starve off those last few pounds and have finally arrived at our ideal weight when suddenly the yo-yo hits the end of its string and jumps back up to the top, each time climbing a little higher. Sound familiar?

It's time to put a stop to it all! Change your life. Throw out all calorie-saving measures. You have to eat to lose weight. And in the future you'll notice that when you fill up your tank with "super," you will feel more energetic, alive, and joyful than you ever dreamed possible. The following five principles will guide you on your journey:

1. Carbohydrates with a low-glycemic index let you drop pounds

2. Fat doesn't just turn to fat—you need some fat in your diet

3. Protein melts away the body's extra padding
4. Without vital nutrients, our metabolism grinds to a halt
5. Without exercise, we can't even begin

METABOLISM—THE WHEEL OF LIFE

Your body contains a natural wonder, your metabolism. Think of it as the wheel of life, or a complicated biological system that converts the food you eat to energy, body tissues, creative thoughts, and joyful feelings. You determine all that you are, the way you feel, and the amount of strength and joy you experience each day by what you choose to eat. The only thing is, your system is millions of years old. Four million years ago, our first human ancestor's biological system was programmed to run on a naturally pure diet of lean meat, fruits, roots, vegetables, and grains. Our system has remained the same but the fuel has changed dramatically. Up to 75% of what we eat is a product of industry. Admittedly, these days no one wants to sit in the kitchen, plucking
a chicken. Being able to take our vegetables from the freezer saves us time and encourages good health. At the same time, however, we overload our bodies with substances that our genes don't recognize. There's no genetic program for metabolizing instant soups, ketchup, candy bars, and the like. The body strives in vain to defend itself, contracting illnesses of civilization such as obesity, diabetes, gout, heart disease, chronic fatigue, depression, and cancer.

THE WRONG FUEL

If we treated our cars in the same way we treat our bodies, they would never even make it out of the garage. From morning 'till night we fill our tanks with the worst kind of fuel, even though we know this destroys the engine: Fast food and chocolate, white flour and sugar, preservatives and dyes, artificial additives and contaminants—all of them unfamiliar to our metabolism. Larger amounts of these substances throw off the delicate balance of hormones in our bodies. As a result we become fat—and unhappy. But we can take precautionary measures by avoiding processed products. Excessive weight is our body's response to a lack of vital nutrients. Packaged foods often contain a hodgepodge of dead nutrients, supplemented with 7000 flavorings and a few token vitamins to promote sales.

HOW TO LOSE WEIGHT

Give your body's 70 billion cells the vital nutrients, basic materials, and energy they need and they will thank you with a lively dance of hormones, a powerful immune system, firm muscles, nerves of steel, active organs, and an attractive figure. If you neglect even one nutrient, your body will respond with fatigue, bad moods, dull hair, and extra pounds. It is a lack of certain nutrients that makes you fat. It is nutrients that help burn off the fat. Nutrients are the fat burners.

Low-Glycemic

Warning— sugar is stronger than your will!

Carbohydrates

Carbohydrates come from such diverse sources as sugar and honey, chocolate, candy, whole-grain bread, fruits, and vegetables. The difference between them is that some of these foods make us fatter, while others are true fat burners that melt off the pounds. It all depends on their glycemic index.

THE GLYCEMIC INDEX

The glycemic index is your fate. It determines whether you will be fat or thin. The glycemic index formula is simple: Carbohydrates that raise your blood sugar (in other words, those that enter your bloodstream rapidly) have a glycemic index of over 50, meaning that they have the potential to make you fat. These include sugar, sweetened beverages, polished rice, white flour, chips, and many more pro-cessed products (see table on page 5). Low-glycemic foods (those with an index of under 50) stabilize your blood sugar level and are genuine fat burners. These include the natural carbohydrates derived from fruits, vegetables, and whole-grain products.

THE POWER OF SUGAR

Whenever you eat, you trigger a dance of hormones in your body. These hormones control your energy metabolism. They either deposit the fat on your hips or take it off and transport it to the mitochondria, tiny kilns in your cells that combust the fat into heat. Glucagon, for example, is a fat-burning hormone. Insulin, on the other hand, is a fat storer. Whenever you eat a high-glycemic food such as candy, white flour, or polished rice, the sugar molecules quickly pass from the intestines to the bloodstream. Your pancreas doesn't have a clue about what is happening, since refined food wasn't introduced until 500 years ago, so it panics. It dispatches an entire armada of insulin to halt the advancing sugar barrage. The insulin either diverts the sugar from the blood stream to the muscles or converts it to fat on your hips. Your blood sugar drops dramatically and rapidly and your brain's sugar supply is depleted. If you have no more sugar in your blood, you lose the ability to concentrate. You become distracted, nervous, and tired. Your brain feels threatened and soon responds with a ravenous craving for something sweet. And you give it what it wants because sugar is stronger than your will. And the problem is, if you start your day with sugar you won't be able to end it without sugar.

INSULIN WEIGHT GAIN

Carbohydrate craving is a phenomenon that causes people to gain weight. Usually, quick carbohydrates are combined with fat, whether in chocolate bars or chips. The insulin created by eating these substances sends the fat straight to your fat cells where it gets locked away. As long as insulin dominates your blood, glucagon, the fat-burning hormone, doesn't have a chance. As soon as you change your diet to fat burners, foods with a low-glycemic index, glucagon will take over and send the fat to your muscles to be combusted. As for high-glycemic foods, enjoy them in moderation and try not to combine them with fat.

FAT STORERS—
HIGH-GLYCEMIC FOODS

Beverages: Beer 110; soft drinks, colas, sweetened fruit juices 80–100

Sweeteners: Honey 75; sugar 75; chocolate 70; jellies and jams 60

Bread: White sandwich bread 95; pretzels 85; French bread 70; mixed-grain rye bread 65

Potatoes: Fried potatoes 95; mashed potatoes 90; french fries 80; boiled potatoes 65

Fruits and vegetables: Carrots 85; winter squash 75; corn 70; watermelon 70; pineapple 65; raisins 65; bananas 60; honeydew melon 60

Grain products: Cornflakes, popcorn 85; rice cakes, puffed rice 80; sweetened muesli 70; corn chips 75; crackers 75; croissants 70; cornmeal 70; wheat flour 70; instant rice 90; polished white rice 70; couscous 60; pasta 60

FAT BURNERS—
LOW-GLYCEMIC FOODS

Sweeteners: Unsweetened jam 30; fruit-flavored ice cream (unsweetened, homemade) 35; unsweetened chocolate (over 70% cocoa) 20

Bread: Whole-wheat or bran bread 50; pumpernickel 40; whole rye bread 40

Fruits and vegetables: Fresh vegetables 15; mushrooms 15; fresh vegetable juices 15; fresh fruits 10–30; freshly squeezed fruit juices (unsweetened) 40; dried apricots 30; soybeans 15; lentils 30; peas 50

Grain products: Whole-grain unsweetened muesli 40; oatmeal 40; rye 35; whole-grain rice 50; whole-grain pasta 30

Miscellaneous: Whole-milk dairy products approx. 35; low-fat milk 30; plain unsweetened yogurt 15; nuts 15–30

Fat Alone

The right fats burn off unwanted padding

is not the Enemy

You need fat to burn fat. Even the most scorned fattener is actually a fat burner. Studies show that athletes who avoid all fat will suddenly gain weight while their muscles shrink. And no wonder! Essential fatty acids are as important as vitamins. Without them, your body is unable to produce fat-burning hormones. Fat isn't just your number one source of energy; it calms your nerves, builds your cells, makes your skin smooth and youthful, and cushions your organs and nerves—and without fat, you wouldn't be able to produce any hormones.

EAT HALF THE FAT— AND CHANGE THE TYPE

Obviously you can't subvert the laws of conservation of energy. Energy doesn't just disappear. Whatever you put into your body and don't burn off in your muscles makes a stopover in your fat cells. Consuming about 60 to 70 fat grams per day will keep you lean and fit, provided they don't all come from saturated animal fats. Animal fat should be kept to a minimum; it is not a fat burner. You're better off consuming unsaturated fatty acids. These are substances your body can't produce on its own. Good sources are vegetables, olives, nuts, seeds, and fish.

FATS THAT KEEP YOU THIN

Your kitchen should always contain olive oil, the traditional oil of the slender centenarians living on the Isle of Crete. Olive oil supplies fatty acids that adjust the settings of your hormone balance to Lean, Fit, and Healthy. The same can be said of the omega-3 fatty acids found in fish. They control your body's super-hormones, the eicosanoids. If you eat ocean fish (such as herring, salmon, or mackerel) at least twice a week, you will stimulate a good number of these types of eicosanoids that will in turn give you better health, more vitality, a lighter mood, and protection for your heart.

FAT AND HIGH-GLYCEMIC INDEX

If you eat your pasta with a cream sauce or your roast beef with mashed potatoes, the potatoes and pasta (both have a high-glycemic index) will increase the insulin in your blood, which will then immediately transport the fat in the beef or cream to your hips, and seal away the fat molecules inside the fat cells. This won't happen, however, if you eat your meat with whole-wheat pasta (low-glycemic index). In this case the insulin is kept at bay, and the fat from the meat can be burned off in the muscle cells. When planning you meals, remember the following:

* Avoid eating fatty foods with high-glycemic foods (steak with French fries, pasta with cream sauce, buttered bread with jam, pizza, chocolate croissants, white bread with cheese that is over 40% fat).

* Create fat-burning combinations: Lamb with whole-grain rice, turkey breast with boiled potatoes, chicken with vegetables, whole-wheat pasta with shrimp, mozzarella, or whole-wheat bread with tomatoes.

THE THIN COMMANDMENTS

* Use olive oil instead of animal fats. Use less butter, cream, and margarine.

* Practice "light" cooking: Brush oil onto non-stick pans for sautéing. Choose steaming and braising to preserve vitamins and your figure.

* Eat things with zero fat: Legumes, fruits, fresh fruits, and whole grains (rice, pasta, bread, muesli) contain little or no fat.

* Reduce your consumption of red meats and processed meats like sausage or bacon. Instead choose ocean fish, game, and poultry. Choose lean cuts of meat: Fillets, escalopes, and loins.

* Always purchase low-fat dairy products and avoid prepared products, even if they say "light." Nature always does it better.

Power from Protein
Make those pounds disappear as if by magic
and Vital Nutrients

Nature provides you with a miracle substance that takes off the pounds while you eat: Protein. Protein does this for two reasons:
1. Your body devotes a great deal of its energy to converting dietary protein to valuable body materials such as muscles, hormones, your immune system, materials for repairing cells, promoting youthfulness, and vitality. It does so by availing itself of stored fat. This makes protein a real fat burner.
2. Muscles and fat-burning hormones are made up of protein. If you don't consume 50 to 100 grams of this high-power fuel every day you will lose valuable muscle mass, become sluggish and consequently, gain weight. But don't look to red meats and processed meats as your protein source. These foods supply purines, artery-damaging cholesterol, and saturated animal fats. Healthy sources of protein are fish, poultry, legumes, and low-fat dairy products.

TOO LITTLE PROTEIN AND VITAL NUTRIENTS MAKE YOU FAT

Protein must be broken down in your stomach and intestines into its tiny building blocks, the amino acids. This is the only way this valuable material can be transported to the cells, fortify your immune system, and help build fat-burning hormones, muscles, nerves and organs. If vital nutrients aren't present, however, the protein remains in your intestines without doing its job. It doesn't serve as a fat burner or high-power fuel for your body. As a result, many people suffer from a lack of protein.

Obesity is your body's response to too many "dead" nutrients and not enough vital nutrients. Vitamins and minerals act as the agents of energy metabolism. If they aren't present, fat can't be broken down and protein can't be utilized, and converted to muscles and fat-burning hormones. In other words, you put on more and more weight.

THE SIX RULES OF SLIMNESS

1. Live naturally: Consume the fat burners available from nature. Every day eat five servings of fruits and vegetables. Snack on seeds and nuts, preferably raw. Reach for whole-grain and dairy products. Eat fish three to five times a week.

2. Get enough vitamin C: Ensure that you are getting enough vitamin C, which the body uses to break down fat. Citrus fruits are good sources or opt for a supplement.

3. Consider a nutritional supplement: Due to modern methods of food production, little that is healthy remains in our foods. Fill up your empty tank with high-quality vitamin and mineral supplement. Be conscious of the vital nutrients that burn fat: Calcium, magnesium, chromium, iodine, selenium, and B vitamins.

4. Eat fitness-promoting combinations: Always combine protein (dairy products, meat, and fish) with carbohydrates (vegetables, salad, and fruit). This will provide you with both the vitamins you need for protein metabolism and the sugar you need for your brain. It will force your body to use its cushion of fat, to convert the protein contained in foods into energy.

5. Stock up on protein: You need at least 0.4 grams of protein per pound of bodyweight. If you consume one serving of protein every four hours, you will always have enough materials to produce the fat-burning hormones STH (growth hormone) and norepinephrine.

6. Never skip a meal: If you don't have time to make a full meal, mix up a protein shake. Look for prepared mixes at a health food store. Instead of satisfying your hunger with an unhealthy sandwich, shake up a skinny drink and accompany it with fresh fruit.

LOW-FAT SOURCES OF PROTEIN

4 oz contains	g of fat	4 oz contains	g of fat
MILK & DAIRY PRODUCTS		**FISH**	
Buttermilk	0.5	Pike perch, sole, pollack	1
Cheddar	32	Salmon	14
Cottage cheese	2.9	Shrimp	1.4
Cream cheese, low-fat	0.3	Trout	3
Edam	28	Yellow perch	0.8
Feta	16		
Goat cheese	21	**MEAT AND POULTRY**	
Kefir	3.5	Chicken	2
Milk, low-fat	2	Corned beef	6
Mozzarella	16.1	Fillet of beef	4
Parmesan	25	Fillet of veal	1
Yogurt, low-fat	0.1	Ham	3
		Poultry sausage	5
FISH		Rabbit	3
Bismarck herring (filleted pickled herring)	16	Roast beef	5
Cod	0.8	Saddle of venison	4
Crayfish	1.1	Turkey breast	1
Flounder	2		
Lobster	1.9	**MISCELLANEOUS**	
Mackerel, smoked	16	Eggs	5.2
Mussels	1.3	Legumes, grains	Trace
Oysters	1.2	Tofu	5
Pike	0.9		

Power

Lose up to seven pounds in seven days with the glycemic index formula

Week

If you use the recipes in this book and follow the rules below, you can melt off a pound a day.

1. Exercise: Run or walk 30 minutes every morning on an empty stomach and at a moderate pace with a fat-burning pulse of around 130. Keep track with a pulse monitor. Breathe in for four steps and out for four steps, breathing deeply and regularly. And if the pulse monitor alarm goes off, slow down until you feel like speeding up again. Run once more in the evening.

2. Drink: Drink 3 quarts of water with fresh lemon juice every day. Drinking a 16-ounce glass of water after dessert and before leaving the table aids digestion. Avoid all drinks containing sugar as well as beer (high-glycemic index). A single glass of dry white wine is OK.

3. Eat: Eat fat-burning combinations regularly. If you need to skip a meal, shake up a protein drink instead and eat some fresh fruit.

4. Pre-eat: Before every meal, eat a large bowl of salad. Feel free to take a larger portion of whole-grain rice or pasta.

5. Train: Buy a latex exercise band with instructions. Exercise problem areas for 10 to 20 minutes, including your abdomen, hips, and buns. Your body will then form fat-burning muscles and hormones.

6. Avoid the scale: Measure your progress by the fit of your jeans rather than by the scale. You're in the process of reducing fat and building muscles, which are heavier than fat.

7. Avoid sweets: Snack on a bar of unsweetened chocolate, which has a low-glycemic index. A spoonful of fat burning Three Berry Jam will also do the trick (recipe on page 15). If you just can't stop thinking about chocolate, go running. The change of scene will redirect your thoughts.

AND AFTER THE FITNESS WEEK?

There is no "after." You will run and eat your way to a new, thin, active life. Use sugar like a spice, avoid white flour as much as possible. You don't have to practice total self-denial. It's a matter of what you do throughout the 365 days of the year. Just keep eating a lot of fat burners.

Power Week

Monday

* Apple-Raspberry Muesli with Kefir ✽ Tomato Stuffed with Radish Yogurt
* Zucchini Strips with Cured Salmon
* Spaghetti with Herb Pesto

Tuesday

* Whole-Wheat Rolls with Tomato ✽ Strawberries with Two Dips
* Artichoke-Cherry Tomato Salad
* Monkfish Ragout with Lentils

Wednesday

* Berry-Pistachio Yogurt ✽ Citrus-Spiked Fat Burner Drink
* Chicken Skewers with Cucumber-Radish Salad
* Oven Ratatouille with Millet

Thursday

* Radish-Cheese Spread on Pumpernickel ✽ Raspberry-Mango Salad
* Marinated Asparagus with Turkey
* Sole with Spring Vegetables

Friday

* Bread with Three-Berry Jam ✽ Tomato Bell Pepper Mix
* Seafood Cocktail with Broccoli
* Boiled Potatoes with Veggie-Garlic Dip

Saturday

* Avocado with Tomato Cottage Cheese ✽ Blackberry Sherbet
* Kohlrabi and Mushroom Carpaccio
* Tuna Skewers with Saffron Rice

Sunday

* Tropical Fruits with Coconut-Lime Yogurt ✽ Arugula Dip with Crispbread
* Tomato-Apple Salad with Arugula
* Bean Sprout and Chicken Stir-Fry

Berry-Pistachio Yogurt

Start your day with

fruit and protein

Serves 2: • 9 oz mixed berries or grapes • 2 tsp lemon juice • 1 tbs apple juice concentrate • 4 tsp pistachio nuts • 1 1/4 cups plain low-fat yogurt

Rinse the fruit briefly, drain and sort. Cut large fruit into smaller pieces. Toss the berries with the lemon juice and apple juice concentrate. Chop the pistachios and stir them into the yogurt. In small glass dishes, arrange alternating layers of berries and yogurt, saving 1/3 of the berries for sprinkling on top.

power

POWER PER SERVING: 151 CALORIES • 7 G PROTEIN • 5 G FAT • 21 G CARBOHYDRATES

Tropical Fruits with
The selenium in coconut makes you cheerful
Coconut-Lime Yogurt

Serves 2: • 1 papaya • 1 star fruit (whole foods market or Latin market) • 1 kiwi • 1 cup low-fat vanilla yogurt

• 2 tbs unsweetened coconut milk • 2 tsp brown sugar • 1 tbs lime juice • 2 tsp grated coconut, toasted

Peel the papaya, remove the seeds and slice. Wash and slice the star fruit. Peel the kiwi and cut

it into wedges. Arrange the fruit decoratively on a plate. Mix the yogurt with the coconut milk,

sugar, and lime juice. Drizzle the coconut mixture over the fruit or serve it in a bowl alongside.

Garnish with the grated coconut.

POWER PER SERVING: 170 CALORIES • 14 G PROTEIN • 2 G FAT • 23 G CARBOHYDRATES

Apple-Raspberry Muesli
A real brain food combination
with Kefir

Serves 2: • 2 tbs pumpkin seeds • 4 tbs rolled oats • 1 tbs raisins • 1 apple • 1 tbs lemon juice

• 4 oz fresh raspberries • 1 1/2 cups kefir (natural foods store) • 2 tsp maple syrup

Toast the pumpkin seeds, and mix them with the oats and raisins. Divide the mixture among

two small bowls. Peel the apple and grate it, avoiding the core. Toss the grated apple with the

lemon juice. Briefly rinse the raspberries, removing any foreign matter. Mix the kefir and maple

syrup. Sprinkle the apples and raspberries over the oat mixture, and pour the kefir over the top.

POWER PER SERVING: 280 CALORIES • 12 G PROTEIN • 10 G FAT • 34 G CARBOHYDRATES

Bread with

Fat burner jam to feed your sweet tooth

Three-Berry Jam

Rinse the berries briefly, sort and trim them, and cut into small pieces. In a saucepan, simmer the berries, fructose, and ascorbic acid for 5 minutes over low heat.

Stir the agar-agar into the cold water, add it to the saucepan, and simmer for an additional 2 to 3 minutes over low heat.

Immediately transfer the berry jam to two small glass canning jars with screw tops, seal them tightly, and let cool. Tip: Sterilize the jars first by boiling the jars and the lids in water for 5 minutes; fill them while still hot.

To eat, spread 1 tbs of the cream cheese and 2 tbs of the jam on each slice of bread. Garnish with mint. Store the remaining jam in the refrigerator and consume as quickly as possible.

Serves 2:
9 oz mixed ripe berries
2 1/2 oz fructose (natural foods store)
1 tsp granulated ascorbic acid
(natural foods store)
1/2 tsp agar-agar
(vegetable gelling agent—
natural foods store)
2 tbs cold water
2 tbs low-fat cream cheese
2 slices whole-wheat bread
1 sprig fresh mint

Whole-Wheat Bread

White bread has a high-glycemic index and is a true fat storer. On the other hand, most whole-grain breads are fat burners. Whenever possible, spread your whole-wheat bread with low-fat cream cheese as an accompaniment to jam instead of butter. Whole-wheat bread is also an excellent accompaniment to vegetables and salad.

POWER PER SERVING:

240 CALORIES

5 G PROTEIN • 2 G FAT

52 G CARBOHYDRATES

power

Whole-Wheat Rolls

The secret to eternal youth from Crete

with Tomato

Thoroughly mash the herb paté with a fork and mix it with the tomato paste, lemon juice, and olive oil until smooth. Season to taste with pepper and salt.

Serves 2:
1/4 cup vegetarian herb paté (natural foods store)
3 tsp tomato paste (preferably organic)
1 tsp lemon juice
1 tsp olive oil
Black pepper to taste
Salt to taste
2 whole-wheat rolls
2 tomatoes
2 sprigs fresh basil

Slice the rolls in half horizontally, and spread the paté mixture on all of the halves, dividing evenly. Wash the tomatoes, remove the cores and cut them into small wedges.

Arrange the tomato wedges on the roll halves. Sprinkle with a little salt and pepper. Wash the basil, shake it dry, pull off the leaves and use them to garnish the rolls.

Tomatoes

Tomatoes raise your spirits, are tonic for your heart and liver, and help prevent gout and rheumatism. They contain the antioxidant lycopene, which helps prevent cancer. Tomatoes also contain minerals that stimulate fat burning, including magnesium, calcium, iron, and zinc. They also contain potassium, which is a natural diuretic.

16

POWER PER SERVING:

196 CALORIES

8 G PROTEIN • 5 G FAT

30 G CARBOHYDRATES

power

Radish-Cheese Spread

Spicy slices of vital nutrients

on Pumpernickel

Serves 2: • 1 tsp butter, softened • 1/2 tsp brown mustard • 2 large slices pumpernickel bread
• 2 oz radishes • 2 oz Camembert cheese • Black pepper to taste • 1 tbs radish sprouts

Mix the butter and mustard, and spread it on the pumpernickel slices. Wash and trim the radishes. Cut the radishes and Camembert into thin slices. Arrange the radishes and Camembert in an overlapping pattern on the bread slices. Season with freshly ground pepper and sprinkle with the radish sprouts.

POWER PER SERVING: 152 CALORIES • 10 G PROTEIN • 6 G FAT • 15 G CARBOHYDRATES

Smoked Salmon with

Fish—a superior fat burner

Horseradish and Apple

Serves 2: • 2 tbs low-fat cream cheese • 1 tsp grated fresh horseradish • Black pepper to taste
• 1/4 medium apple • 2 tsp lemon juice • 2 slices dark rye bread • 2 sprigs fresh dill • 2 oz smoked salmon

Mix the cream cheese with the horseradish and a little pepper. Wash the apple, cut it into thin slices, and immediately drizzle it with the lemon juice. Spread the horseradish mixture on the bread slices and cut them in half diagonally. Wash the dill and shake it dry. Arrange the apple slices, smoked salmon, and dill sprigs on the bread, dividing evenly.

POWER PER SERVING: 158 CALORIES • 10 G PROTEIN • 6 G FAT • 15 G CARBOHYDRATES

Avocado with

A recipe for beauty, a slender figure, and healthy nerves

Tomato Cottage Cheese

Wash and quarter the tomato, remove the seeds and core, and cut it into small cubes. Cut the avocado in half and remove the pit. Scoop out the avocado flesh from the peel with a large spoon, leaving only a thin outer layer inside the peel halves and dice the flesh. Immediately drizzle the lemon juice over the avocado halves and diced avocado. Mix the cottage cheese with the diced tomato and diced avocado. Season with a little salt and pepper. Transfer the mixture to the hollowed-out avocado halves, sprinkle with the chopped chives, and serve.

Serves 2:

1 tomato

1 ripe avocado

2 tsp fresh lemon juice

1/2 cup cottage cheese

Salt to taste

Black pepper to taste

1 tbs chopped fresh chives

Avocados

Although this green exotic is the fattiest of fruits, it is loaded with unsaturated fatty acids that are essential to a healthy diet. They promote soft skin, healthy cell walls and strong nerves, and program your body's hormones to burn fat. Eat avocados and the fat storing hormone, insulin doesn't stand a chance.

POWER PER SERVING:

394 CALORIES

10 G PROTEIN • 38 G FAT

2 G CARBOHYDRATES

Raw Vegetables with

Dip into vitality

Herbed Cream Cheese

Mix together the cream cheese, mineral water, lemon juice, salt and pepper, and stir until smooth. Peel and mince the garlic. Wash the parsley, shake it dry, and set several leaves aside. Finely chop the remaining parsley leaves. Stir the chopped parsley and garlic into the cream cheese mixture.

Trim and wash the radishes. Trim and wash the celery and cut it into slices. Cut the bell pepper in half and remove the stem, ribs, and seeds, then wash it and cut it into strips. Cut the bread into little triangles. Decoratively arrange the radishes, celery, and pepper strips around the dip. Garnish with the remaining parsley leaves and serve with the bread triangles.

Serves 2:

4 oz low-fat cream cheese

2 tbs mineral water

2 tsp lemon juice

Salt to taste

Black pepper to taste

1 clove garlic

1/4 bunch fresh Italian parsley

4 oz radishes

2 stalks celery

1 small yellow bell pepper

1 slice whole rye bread

POWER PER SERVING: 122 CALORIES • 11 G PROTEIN • 1 G FAT • 16 G CARBOHYDRATES

Arugula Dip

Triggers a flood of "happiness hormones"

with Crispbread

Serves 2: • 3 oz arugula • 2 tbs pumpkin seeds • 2 tbs freshly grated Parmesan cheese
• 2 tsp balsamic vinegar • 2 tbs olive oil • 4–5 tbs vegetable stock • Salt to taste • Balck pepper to taste
• 1 green onion • 2 slices rye crispbread

Trim, sort, wash, and chop the arugula. Place the arugula, pumpkin seeds, Parmesan, vinegar, and olive oil in a blender or food processor, and process to a smooth purée. Stir in the stock to form a creamy paste, and season with salt and pepper. Wash and trim the green onion, slice it into fine rings, and add it to the paste. Break up the crispbread and use it for dipping.

POWER PER SERVING: 262 CALORIES • 9 G PROTEIN • 22 G FAT • 11 G CARBOHYDRATES

Bell Pepper

Fat-burning enzymes do their part

Pineapple Salsa

Serves 2: • 10 oz pineapple • 1/2 red bell pepper • 1/2 small red onion • 1 tbs lime juice • Salt to taste
• Tabasco sauce to taste • 2 tsp olive oil • 1 tbs chopped fresh cilantro • Whole-wheat toast

Peel the pineapple and cut it into small cubes, avoiding the tough core. Wash and trim the bell pepper, and dice it finely. Peel the onion and chop it finely. Stir together the pineapple, bell pepper, onion, lime juice, salt, Tabasco, olive oil, and cilantro. Serve with the whole-wheat toast.

POWER PER SERVING: 95 CALORIES • 1 G PROTEIN • 5 G FAT • 12 G CARBOHYDRATES

Tomato Stuffed with
Essential oils keep you fit
Radish Yogurt

Serves 2: • 2 large, ripe tomatoes • 4 oz radishes • 3/4 cup plain nonfat yogurt •
• 2 tbs chopped fresh chives • Salt to taste • Black pepper to taste • 1 tsp lemon juice

Wash the tomatoes. Slice off the top of each tomato and scoop out the tomato flesh with a spoon (save the flesh for another use, if desired). Wash and grate the radishes. Mix the grated radishes with the yogurt and 1 tbs of the chives. Season the mixture with salt, pepper, and lemon juice. Fill the tomatoes with the radish yogurt and sprinkle with the remaining chives.

POWER PER SERVING: 64 CALORIES • 5 G PROTEIN • 1 G FAT • 9 G CARBOHYDRATES

Zucchini Rounds
A deposit in your health account
with Mushrooms

Serves 2: • 3 oz white mushrooms • 1 green onion • 2 tsp fresh lemon juice • 1 tsp balsamic vinegar
• 1 1/2 tbs olive oil • Salt to taste • Black pepper to taste • 8 oz large zucchini

Trim, wash, and slice the mushrooms and green onion. Mix them with the lemon juice, vinegar, 1 tbs of the olive oil, salt, and pepper. Trim and wash the zucchini, cut it into 8 slices and season with salt. Brush the remaining oil in a skillet and heat to medium. Sauté the zucchini slices for a few minutes on both sides, and season with salt and pepper. Place the zucchini on serving plates and top with the mushrooms.

POWER PER SERVING: 87 CALORIES • 3 G PROTEIN • 7 G FAT • 3 G CARBOHYDRATES

Ham-Wrapped

These slender stalks are true fat burners

Asparagus with Basil Dip

Wash the asparagus, break off the woody ends, and peel the bottom third of the stalks. In a saucepan, bring a generous amount of salted water to a boil with the oil. Add the asparagus, cover, reduce the heat, and simmer until tender-crisp, about 10 to 12 minutes.

Serves 2:
10 oz asparagus
Salt to taste
1 tsp olive oil
1/2 cup plain low-fat yogurt
2 tbs sour cream
1 tsp small capers (drained)
1 tsp fresh lemon juice
Black pepper to taste
12 fresh basil leaves
2 oz lean smoked ham

For the dip, mix the yogurt and sour cream. Finely chop the capers and mix them in. Season the dip with lemon juice, salt, and pepper. Wash and shake dry the basil leaves and set several leaves aside. Chop the remaining leaves finely and mix them into the dip. Drain the asparagus, plunge it into ice water to stop the cooking, and drain again.

Wrap the ham around the asparagus and arrange on a platter. Garnish the dip with the remaining basil.

Lighten Up Your Sauces

One-half cup of cream contains 31 fat grams and the same amount of crème fraîche contains 40 grams. Instead of using these ingredients, try lightening up your sauces. Try, for example, puréed vegetables, which have a delicate taste and a smooth texture. Or you can replace the cream with low-fat buttermilk, sour cream, or yogurt.

POWER PER SERVING:

185 CALORIES

9 G PROTEIN • 14 G FAT

6 G CARBOHYDRATES

Cucumber-Shrimp

The best fat burners come from the sea

Salad

Serves 2:
1/4 cup frozen peas
2 tsp sunflower kernels
Salt to taste
7 oz cucumber
4 oz peeled cooked shrimp
2 red leaf lettuce leaves
1/4 bunch fresh dill
1/2 cup kefir (natural foods store)
1 tsp fresh lemon juice
1 tsp canola oil
Black pepper to taste
Pumpernickel crackers

Thaw the peas. In an ungreased skillet, toast the sunflower kernels until golden brown. Peel, dice, and lightly salt the cucumber. Rinse the shrimp and drain. Wash the lettuce, shake it dry, and tear it into bite-sized pieces. Wash the dill, shake it dry, and set aside 2–3 sprigs. Remove the leaves from the remaining sprigs and chop. In a large bowl, stir together the kefir, lemon juice, and canola oil until smooth. Season with salt and pepper. Add the peas, cucumber, shrimp, lettuce, and dill to the bowl and toss well. Divide the salad among serving plates, sprinkle with sunflower seeds, garnish with the remaining dill, and serve with pumpernickel crackers.

Shrimps for Taurine

Shrimp provides taurine, a protein substance that helps the pituitary gland to send out its fat melting hormones, such as the growth hormone that builds up muscles and breaks down fat. This valuable fat burner can also be found in mussels, poultry, and liver.

POWER PER SERVING:

166 CALORIES

14 G PROTEIN • 6 G FAT

14 G CARBOHYDRATES

Raspberry-Mango Salad

Snack yourself to slenderness

Serves 2: • 1 ripe mango • 6 oz fresh raspberries • 1/2 cup low-fat cottage cheese • 1/2 cup plain low-fat yogurt • 1 tsp honey • 2 tsp pine nuts, toasted • 1 sprig fresh mint

Peel the mango, cut thin wedges away from the pit, and arrange them on a serving dish. Rinse the raspberries briefly, sort them, and sprinkle them over the mango wedges. Stir together the cottage cheese, yogurt, and honey and pour over the top. Sprinkle with pine nuts. Wash the mint, remove the leaves from the stem, and use them to garnish the salad.

POWER PER SERVING: 199 CALORIES • 6 G PROTEIN • 7 G FAT • 23 G CARBOHYDRATES

Blackberry Sherbet

A craving for ice cream? Go right ahead!

Serves 2: • 9 oz fresh blackberries • 2 tsp lemon juice • 1 tbs maple syrup • 1/4 cup water • 1 sprig fresh mint

Wash and drain the blackberries. Set a few berries aside and purée the rest together with the lemon juice, maple syrup, and water. Place the blackberry purée in a stainless steel bowl, cover, and freeze 3–4 hours, stirring at 1-hour intervals. Transfer the sherbet to dessert bowls, and garnish with the remaining berries and mint.

POWER PER SERVING: 82 CALORIES • 2 G PROTEIN • 1 G FAT • 14 G CARBOHYDRATES

Strawberries

Fruit for your sweet tooth

with Two Dips

Rinse, sort, and drain the strawberries.

For the chocolate dip, chop the chocolate coarsely.
Place it in a bowl with 3 tbs of the milk. In a double
boiler, that is hot but not boiling, melt the chocolate
over low heat while stirring constantly. Let the
chocolate dip cool.

For the vanilla dip, slit open the vanilla bean
lengthwise, scrape out the seeds with a small knife,
and mix them with the honey, the remaining 1 tbs
milk, and the yogurt.

Arrange the strawberries decoratively on a plate,
and serve them with the chocolate and vanilla dips.

Serves 2:
9 oz fresh strawberries
1 1/2 oz unsweetened chocolate
1/4 cup low-fat milk
1/2 vanilla bean
1 tsp floral honey
1/4 cup low-fat vanilla yogurt

power

POWER PER SERVING:

158 CALORIES

7 G PROTEIN • 5 G FAT

20 G CARBOHYDRATES

Kiwi-Strawberry

A sweet fat burner cocktail

Shake with Mint

Serves 2 drinks: • 1 kiwi • 3–4 oz fresh strawberries • 2 tsp chopped fresh mint • Juice from 1 lime • 2 tsp maple syrup • 2 tbs quick-cooking oatmeal • 1/2 cup plain low-fat yogurt • 1/2 cup cold milk

Peel and dice the kiwi. Wash and trim the strawberries and cut them into small pieces. Put the mint, lime juice, maple syrup, oat flakes, and yogurt in a blender and purée for about 15 seconds. Add the milk and purée vigorously once again. Pour into two large glasses and serve with wide straws.

POWER PER DRINK: 83 CALORIES • 2 G PROTEIN • 1 G FAT • 17 G CARBOHYDRATES

Tomato

A spicy fat burner cocktail

Bell Pepper Mix

Serves 2 drinks: • 3 oz red bell pepper • 3 oz celery root (celeriac) • 2 tbs chopped fresh Italian parsley • 1/2 tsp red chile flakes • 1 1/4 cups cold tomato juice • Salt to taste • Black pepper to taste • 4 ice cubes

Trim and wash the bell pepper, peel the celery root, and dice both vegetables. Put the pepper, celery root, parsley, chile flakes, and 1/2 cup of the tomato juice in a blender and purée. Add the remaining juice and purée vigorously. Season with salt and pepper. Fill 2 glasses with ice cubes, pour the mixture over the top, and serve with wide straws.

POWER PER DRINK: 50 CALORIES • 3 G PROTEIN • 1 G FAT • 8 G CARBOHYDRATES

Citrus-Spiked
The slimming power of tropical fruits
Fat Burner Drink

Plunge the tomatoes into boiling water for a few seconds, transfer them to ice water, drain, and pull off the tomato skins. Cut the tomatoes in half and squeeze out the seeds. Chop the tomatoes coarsely. Trim the carrot, peel, and grate it finely. Remove the seeds from the papaya half, peel, and dice it. Put the tomatoes, carrot, and papaya in a blender. Squeeze the juice from the oranges and lemon, and add to the blender. Add the fructose, ascorbic acid, and olive oil. Blend for 15 seconds at high speed.

Pour the drink into 2 tall glasses. Slit the lemon slices and place on the rim of each glass. Serve with wide straws.

Serves 2 drinks:
2 ripe tomatoes
1 medium carrot
1/2 ripe papaya
2 oranges
1 lemon
1 tsp fructose
(natural foods store)
Dash of ascorbic acid granules
(natural foods store)
1 tsp olive oil
2 slices lemon

Tropical Fruits for Enzymes

Papaya, pineapple, and mango provide enzymes that indirectly boost fat burning. These enzymes break down protein and help transport valuable fat burners to your cells where they do their job of promoting your health and fitness.

POWER PER DRINK:

153 CALORIES

4 G PROTEIN • 3 G FAT

32 G CARBOHYDRATES

Artichoke-Cherry Tomato Salad

Essential fatty acids trigger fat-burning hormones

Add the lemon juice to a medium bowl of water. Break the stems off the artichokes. Cut off the top third of the artichoke leaves. Pull out the inner leaves and the inedible fuzzy center to expose the heart. Trim the hearts and immediately place them in the lemon water.

For the salad dressing, whisk together the vinegar, herb salt, and pepper. With a whisk, gradually beat in the olive oil, canola oil, and sunflower oil.

Drain the artichoke hearts, cut them into very thin strips, and mix them with the dressing.

Meanwhile, peel the shallot and garlic, and chop both finely. Wash the cherry tomatoes, cut larger ones in half, and remove the stems. Add the shallot, garlic, tomatoes, capers, and parsley to the bowl with the artichokes and mix well. Season the salad generously with salt and pepper.

Serves 2:

Juice of 1/2 lemon

2 small artichokes (about 18 oz)

1 1/2 tbs white wine vinegar

Herb salt to taste

Black pepper to taste

2 tbs olive oil

1 tsp canola oil

1 tsp sunflower oil

1 shallot

1 clove garlic

8 oz cherry tomatoes

1 tsp capers (drained)

2 tbs chopped fresh Italian parsley

POWER PER SERVING: 217 CALORIES • 3 G PROTEIN • 18 G FAT • 13 G CARBOHYDRATES

Kohlrabi and
Raw food for nutrition and energy
Mushroom Carpaccio

Serves 2: • 1 tbs sesame seeds • 10 oz kohlrabi • 2 oz mushrooms • 1 green onion • 1 tbs white wine vinegar

• Salt to taste • Black pepper to taste • 2 tbs sunflower oil • 1/2 tsp sesame oil • Whole-wheat bread

In a dry nonstick skillet, toast the sesame seeds. Peel the kohlrabi, cut it into quarters, slice it thinly, and arrange on 2 plates. Clean the mushrooms and cut them into very thin cross sections. Trim the green onion and wash and cut it into rings. Distribute the mushrooms and onion over the kohlrabi. Whisk together the vinegar, salt, pepper, sunflower oil and sesame oil, and drizzle it over the top. Sprinkle with the toasted sesame seeds. Serve with whole-wheat bread.

POWER PER SERVING: 150 CALORIES • 5 G PROTEIN • 12 G FAT • 7 G CARBOHYDRATES

Tomato-Apple Salad
With fat-burning fruits and vegetables
with Arugula

Serves 2: • 4 ripe tomatoes • 1/2 tart apple • 1 carrot • 1 1/2 oz arugula • 1 tbs lemon juice

• 1 tsp balsamic vinegar • Salt to taste • Black pepper to taste • 2 tbs olive oil

• 1 1/2 oz Parmesan cheese • Whole-wheat bread

Wash the tomatoes and cut them into 8 wedges. Cut the apple in half, remove the core, and cut into slices. Peel and grate the carrot. Rinse the arugula, shake dry, remove the stems, and chop. Whisk together lemon juice, vinegar, salt, pepper, and oil. Toss the tomatoes, apple, grated carrot, and arugula with the dressing. With a vegetable peeler, shave the Parmesan over the top. Serve with whole-wheat bread.

POWER PER SERVING: 221 CALORIES • 8 G PROTEIN • 18 G FAT • 8 G CARBOHYDRATES

Tex-Mex Salad

With the fat-burning factor methionine

with Kidney Beans

Rinse and drain the beans. Cut the bell pepper in half and remove the stem, ribs and seeds, and wash and cut it into strips. Cut the avocado in half, then remove the pit and peel. Cut the avocado halves into narrow wedges and immediately drizzle them with the lemon juice. Wash and trim the celery and cut it diagonally into thin slices. Peel the onion, cut it in half, then cut it into half-rings.

Make the dressing: Whisk together the vinegar, salt, pepper, Tabasco, and oil in a medium bowl. Wash the parsley and cilantro, shake it dry, chop it, and add to the dressing. Stir the vegetables into the dressing. Wash the lettuce, shake it dry, and arrange on serving plates. Spoon the vegetables on top of the lettuce leaves.

Serves 2:

4 oz canned red kidney beans (drained)

1 yellow bell pepper

1 avocado

1 tsp lemon juice

1 stalk celery

1 small red onion

2 tbs red wine vinegar

Salt to taste

Pepper to taste

Tabasco sauce to taste

3 tbs extra-virgin olive oil

1/4 bunch fresh cilantro or Italian parsley

4 iceberg lettuce leaves

Legumes for Methionine

Methionine is an important substance for building up protein. A deficiency weakens your immune system, increases your risk for cancer, and causes you to put on weight. Without methionine, there would be no formation of carnitine, which transports fat from your hips to be combusted in your muscles. Good sources of methionine include legumes, fish, poultry, and cheese.

POWER PER SERVING:

377 CALORIES

5 G PROTEIN • 35 G FAT

12 G CARBOHYDRATES

Curried Veal Fillet
with Tomato Yogurt

A hearty way to lose weight

Serves 2:
1 medium tomato
1 small red onion
1 cup plain low-fat yogurt
5 sprigs fresh Italian parsley
Salt to taste
Black pepper to taste
1/2 tsp ground coriander
2 tsp lemon juice
2 cups vegetable stock
7 oz boneless veal
1 tsp curry powder
Dark rye bread

Wash the tomato, cut it in half, squeeze out the seeds, and dice the flesh finely. Peel the onion and dice it finely. Mix together the tomatoes, onion, and yogurt. Wash the parsley, shake it dry, chop it finely, and mix half of it into the tomato yogurt. Season with salt, pepper, coriander, and lemon juice; cover and refrigerate.

In a deep-sided skillet, bring the vegetable stock to a boil. Cut the veal into thin slices. Rub each veal piece with a little curry powder and place in the skillet. Reduce the heat to low and simmer the veal for about 5 minutes. Remove the meat, and season with salt and pepper. Sprinkle with the remaining parsley. Serve the veal with the tomato yogurt and dark rye bread.

Sour Helpers

Vinegar and lemon juice are true slenderizers. Eating a salad with vinegar before a meal of fish, or sprinkling lemon juice over a chicken breast or turkey escalope helps your stomach break down protein and helps your body metabolize it better, thus speeding it to its final destination—the 70 billion cells in your body—where it can do its slenderizing work.

POWER PER SERVING

213 CALORIES

27 G PROTEIN • 5 G FAT

13 G CARBOHYDRATES

Marinated Asparagus

Asparagus reduces weight and blood pressure

with Turkey

Serves 2:

18 oz asparagus

Salt to taste

1 egg

2 tsp pine nuts

2 tbs lemon juice

1 tbs white wine vinegar

Black pepper to taste

2 tbs extra-virgin olive oil

4 oz cherry tomatoes

8 fresh basil leaves

2 oz sliced smoked turkey breast

Wash the asparagus, break off the woody ends, and peel just the lower third of the stalks. Bring a pot of salted water to a boil. Add the asparagus, reduce the heat, and simmer until tender-crisp, about 10–12 minutes. Boil the egg for 10 minutes, until it is cooked hard, then plunge it into cold water. In an ungreased skillet, toast the pine nuts until golden brown. Drain the asparagus, setting aside 3 tbs of the asparagus water. For the marinade, whisk together the lemon juice, vinegar, salt, pepper, oil, and reserved asparagus water. Pour the marinade over the asparagus in a shallow dish and refrigerate for 2–3 hours. Peel the egg and cut it into 8 wedges. Wash the tomatoes and cut them in half. Wash and shake dry the basil, and chop the leaves coarsely. Arrange the egg wedges, tomatoes, and turkey breast alongside the asparagus on serving plates. Sprinkle with the pine nuts and basil.

Skinny Sticks

From April to June you can let yourself go and fill up with asparagus. These skinny sticks contain only 15 calories per 4 oz. The asparagine in asparagus stimulates your kidneys, acting as a natural diuretic. Other fat-burning factors in asparagus are fiber, vitamin C, iron, calcium, and iodine.

POWER PER SERVING

260 CALORIES

15 G PROTEIN • 19 G FAT

9 G CARBOHYDRATES

Chicken Skewers with

Poultry + lemon = a perfect fat-burning combination

Cucumber-Radish Salad

Serves 2: • 8 oz boneless, skinless chicken breast • 2 tbs lemon juice • Salt to taste • Black pepper to taste • 2 tbs olive oil • 9 oz cucumber • 9 oz radishes • 1 tsp red chile flakes • 2 tbs chopped fresh Italian parsley

Cut the chicken breast into cubes and thread them onto 2 wooden skewers. In a shallow dish, mix together 1 tbs of the lemon juice, salt, pepper, and 1/2 tbs of the oil. Add the chicken skewers and turn to coat them well with the marinade. Peel the cucumber. Trim and wash the radishes. Cut the cucumber and radishes into slices. Mix together the remaining 1 1/2 tbs lemon juice, 1 1/2 tbs oil, salt, pepper, and the chile flakes. Add the cucumber, radishes and parsley, and toss well. Broil the skewers in the oven for 8–10 minutes. Serve the chicken with the salad.

POWER PER SERVING: 283 CALORIES • 26 G PROTEIN • 16 G FAT • 6 G CARBOHYDRATES

Zucchini Strips

Loaded with omega-3 fatty acids

with Cured Salmon

Serves 2: • 10 oz zucchini • 2 tbs olive oil • Salt to taste • Black pepper to taste • 2 tsp balsamic vinegar • 4 oz sliced cured salmon (gravlax) • 2 tbs plain low-fat yogurt • 2 slices dark whole-grain bread

Wash and trim the zucchini, then cut it lengthwise into thin slices. Brush a nonstick skillet with some of the oil, add the zucchini slices a few at a time, and sauté for 2–3 minutes on both sides over medium heat. Transfer the zucchini to a shallow bowl, sprinkle with salt, pepper, vinegar and the remaining oil, and marinate for 2 hours. Serve with the salmon, yogurt, and bread.

POWER PER SERVING: 300 CALORIES • 17 G PROTEIN • 24 G FAT • 4 G CARBOHYDRATES

Seafood Cocktail

An extra-light feast

with Broccoli

Cut the cod into strips and the squid into pieces. Rinse the mussels, pull off any hairy filaments, and discard any that are open. In a saucepan, bring 1/2 cup water to a boil.

Simmer the fish strips and squid in the water for 2–3 minutes over low heat; remove them from the water and set aside. Place the mussels in the cooking liquid, cover the pot, and simmer until the shells open, about 3–5 minutes. Remove the mussels from the stock and pull the mussel meat from the shells. Discard any unopened mussels.

Trim the broccoli and blanch it for 3 minutes in boiling, salted water. Plunge the broccoli into cold water and drain. Trim the bell pepper, wash it, and cut it into strips. Trim the green onion, wash it, and cut into rings.

In a medium bowl, whisk together the soy sauce, lemon juice, sugar, salt, and pepper. Stir the cilantro, cod strips, squid, mussels, and vegetables into the marinade. Serve with the baguette.

Serves 2:
4 oz cod fillet
4 oz squid rings or tentacles (cleaned)
10 oz fresh mussels (in the shell)
10 oz broccoli
Salt to taste
1 small red bell pepper
1 green onion
2 tbs soy sauce
2 tbs lemon juice
1 tsp brown sugar
Black pepper to taste
1 tbs chopped fresh cilantro or Italian parsley
Whole-wheat baguette

Seafood: The Super Fat Burner

The protein in seafood stimulates fat burning. Seafood provides you with an abundance of tyrosine, an amino acid that your body uses to produce the fat-burning hormones norepinephrine and dopamine. Seafood also provides iodine, the fuel for an active thyroid.

POWER PER SERVING:

159 CALORIES

25 G PROTEIN • 2 G FAT

10 G CARBOHYDRATES

Spaghetti with Herb Pesto

Laced with three herbs

Plunge the tomatoes into boiling water for a few seconds, transfer them to ice water, drain, and pull off the tomato skins. Cut the tomatoes into quarters, remove the seeds, and cut them into small cubes. In a saucepan, bring a generous amount of salted water to a boil, and cook the spaghetti according to the package instructions, until it is al dente. For the pesto, rinse the chervil, parsley, and basil, shake dry, remove the leaves from the stems, and chop them coarsely. Peel and chop the garlic. Put the chervil, parsley, basil, garlic, vinegar almonds, and Parmesan in a blender or food processor. Add 4–6 tbs water from the spaghetti and process into a fine purée. Gradually drizzle in the oil, and season to taste with salt and pepper.

Serves 2:

18 oz tomatoes
Salt to taste
5 oz whole-wheat spaghetti
Handful of fresh chervil
1/4 bunch fresh Italian parsley
6 large fresh basil leaves
1 small clove garlic
2 tsp balsamic vinegar
2 tbs chopped almonds
1 oz Parmesan cheese, grated
2 tbs olive oil
Black pepper to taste

Drain the pasta, put into a warmed serving bowl, and immediately add the diced tomato, salt, and pepper. Add the pesto to taste, toss well, and serve.

Herbs

Herbs magically transform dishes, maintain your health, calm and relax you, stimulate you and keep you thin. Mixing herbs in recipes gives you maximum nutritional benefit. For example, in the pesto above, chervil promotes circulation and aids digestion; parsley activates your metabolism; and basil fortifies and soothes your stomach.

POWER PER SERVING:

434 CALORIES

17 G PROTEIN • 4 G FAT

41 G CARBOHYDRATES

Boiled Potatoes with

High-glycemic and low-fat

Veggie-Garlic Dip

Scrub the potatoes and boil them in salted water until tender, about 20–25 minutes. Remove the stem, ribs and seeds from the bell pepper, and wash

Serves 2:

1 lb small potatoes
Salt to taste
1/2 red bell pepper
4 oz cucumber
2 green onions
1 small clove garlic
8 oz low-fat cream cheese
3 tbs low-fat milk
2 tsp lemon juice
1/2 tsp hot Hungarian paprika
1/4 bunch fresh dill

and cut it into cubes. Peel the cucumber and dice it finely. Trim the green onions, wash, and cut it into fine rings. Peel the garlic and chop it finely. Mix together the cream cheese, milk and lemon juice, and season generously with salt and paprika. Add the diced bell pepper and cucumber, garlic and two-thirds of the green onion. Wash and shake dry the dill, chop all but a few sprigs, and stir it into the cream cheese mixture. Garnish the cream cheese mixture with the remaining green onions and dill. Drain the potatoes, wait until they're cool enough to handle, peel them, and serve with the dip.

Potatoes

Potatoes have a high-glycemic index. Combine them with fat and the insulin weight gain is complete. That's why we suggest you use a lighter version: 100 grams of boiled potatoes have 0.3 grams of fat, French fries fatten your figure with 14.6 fat grams and chips complete the job with 40 grams of fat. To combat their fat-storing potential, eat potatoes with low-fat cream cheese, lean fish, poultry, or vegetables.

POWER PER SERVING:

243 CALORIES

23 G PROTEIN • 1 G FAT

35 G CARBOHYDRATES

Oven Ratatouille

Pamper your body with lots of vegetables

with Millet

Preheat the oven to 450°F. Cut the bell peppers into quarters. Remove the stems, ribs and seeds, and wash and cut them into pieces. Wash and trim the zucchini and eggplant. Cut the zucchini into slices and the eggplant into large cubes. Peel the onion and dice it coarsely. Wash the tomatoes, cut them into quarters, remove the seeds, and cut them into pieces. Peel and chop the garlic.

Grease a casserole with 1 tbs of the oil and heat in the oven for 5 minutes. Put the vegetables in the casserole and season with salt, pepper and the herbes de Provence. Drizzle the vegetables with the remaining 1 tbs oil and the lemon juice. In the meantime, bring 1/2 cup of the stock to a boil and pour it over the vegetables. Bake the vegetables on the middle oven rack for 30 minutes, stirring occasionally.

Bring the remaining stock to a boil, add the millet, and cook for 25 minutes over low heat, until the millet is tender. Stir in the parsley and season with salt and pepper. Serve the cooked millet with the ratatouille.

Serves 2:
1 small red bell pepper
1 small green bell pepper
4 oz zucchini
4 oz eggplant
1/2 medium onion
8 oz Roma tomatoes
2 cloves garlic
2 tbs olive oil
Salt to taste
Black pepper to taste
1 tsp herbes de Provence
1 tbs lemon juice
3/4 cup vegetable stock
2/3 cup millet
2 tbs chopped fresh Italian parsley

POWER PER SERVING: 464 CALORIES • 11 G PROTEIN • 19 G FAT • 61 G CARBOHYDRATES

Gazpacho with
Croutons

Carotenoids in tomatoes and bell peppers keep you fit

Serves 2:
2 slices stale whole-wheat bread
Salt to taste
7 oz tomato
1 small red bell pepper
1 small green bell pepper
4 oz cucumber
1 clove garlic
1 tsp tomato paste
(preferably organic)
1 cup cold tomato juice
3 tbs vegetable stock
2 tsp olive oil
1–2 tsp lemon juice
1 tsp brown sugar
Cayenne pepper to taste

Cut 1 bread slice into cubes, sprinkle with salt, and soak in 1/4 tbs lukewarm water. In the meantime, plunge the tomato into boiling water for a few seconds, transfer it to ice water, drain, and pull off the tomato skins. Cut the tomatoes in half, squeeze out the seeds, and chop the flesh coarsely. Remove the stems, ribs and seeds from the bell peppers, and wash and dice them. Peel the cucumber, cut it in half lengthwise, scrape out the seeds with a spoon and dice. Peel and chop the garlic.

In a blender or food processor, put the soaked bread, tomatoes, garlic, half each of the red pepper, green pepper, and cucumber, the tomato paste, tomato juice, and stock. Add 1 tsp of the olive oil, the lemon juice, sugar, salt, and cayenne pepper. Process until the mixture is smooth. Cover and refrigerate for 1 hour.

Cut the remaining bread slice into small cubes. In a skillet, heat the remaining 1 tbs olive oil over medium heat. Add the bread cubes and sauté until golden brown. Stir the puréed mixture, pour it into 2 soup bowls, and sprinkle with the remaining diced vegetables and the croutons.

POWER PER SERVING: 166 CALORIES • 5 G PROTEIN • 6 G FAT • 22 G CARBOHYDRATES

Risotto with
Stay slim with whole-grain rice
Raw Vegetables

Serves 2:
1 tbs pumpkin seeds
1 2/3 cups vegetable stock
1 onion
1 small clove garlic
1 tbs olive oil
1/2 cup short-grain brown rice
(natural foods store)
Salt to taste
1/4 cup dry white wine
4 oz zucchini
4 oz carrot
Black pepper to taste
1 1/2 oz Swiss cheese, grated

In a dry skillet, toast the pumpkin seeds and let them cool. Heat the stock in a small saucepan until boiling, then keep warm. Peel the onion and garlic and dice finely. In a saucepan, heat the oil over medium heat and sauté the onion and garlic in it until translucent. Add the rice, toast it briefly, while stirring constantly, and season with salt. Add the wine and simmer until it has nearly evaporated. Add about 1/2 cup of the hot vegetable stock to the rice. Cook the rice for 35–40 minutes, stirring occasionally and gradually adding more stock. The rice is done when it is tender, but still has a slight firmness at the center when you bite into a grain.

While the rice is cooking, wash and trim the zucchini. Peel the carrot. Grate both vegetables. When the rice is done, stir the grated vegetables into it, season with salt and pepper, cover, and let stand for 5 minutes. Sprinkle the risotto with the pumpkin seeds and cheese.

Whole-Grain Rice

Fiber, such as found in whole-grain rice, rescues you from insulin weight gain. Enzymes in your intestines break down the starch of rice or grain into sugar molecules. The fiber from the grain hulls keeps the enzymes from doing this too quickly. As a result, sugar enters your bloodstream more slowly and triggers only a little of the fat storing hormone insulin.

POWER PER SERVING:

484 CALORIES

12 G PROTEIN • 18 G FAT

65 G CARBOHYDRATES

Green Garbanzo

Legumes provide lots of fat-burning protein

Bean Stir-Fry

Wash the spinach well, remove the stems, and chop it coarsely. Cut the bell pepper into quarters, remove the stem, ribs and seeds, and wash and cut it into strips. Trim the green onions, wash, and cut it diagonally into pieces. Wash and trim the peas, removing any strings. Peel the ginger and garlic, and chop them finely. In a wok or skillet, heat the oil over high heat and briefly sauté the ginger and garlic in it. Add the pepper strips, peas and green onions, and sauté for about 4 minutes, stirring constantly. Add the spinach, garbanzo beans and stock, and stir-fry for an additional 2–3 minutes. Season to taste with salt, cayenne pepper, and lemon juice. Transfer the mixture to plates and place 1 tbs yogurt in the center of each serving.

Serves 2:

8 oz spinach leaves

1 green bell pepper

5 oz green onions

4 oz sugar snap peas

1 small piece fresh ginger

1 clove garlic

1 tbs canola oil

9 oz cooked garbanzo beans (drained)

3 tbs vegetable stock

Salt to taste

Cayenne pepper to taste

1–2 tsp lemon juice

2 tbs plain low-fat yogurt

Guaranteed Vitamins

Select vegetables that are in season and come from your own region. Always adhere to these basic principles: Buy fresh, use as soon as possible, don't cut up into pieces that are too small, don't soak too long, and cook gently. Follow the traffic light rule: One red, one green, and one yellow vegetable every day. This will guarantee a wide variety of vitamins and phytochemicals in your diet.

POWER PER SERVING:

492 CALORIES

42 G PROTEIN • 13 G FAT

82 G CARBOHYDRATES

Instant
Enjoy light pizza
Veggie Pizza

For the dough, quickly knead together the yogurt, flour, baking powder, milk, 2 tbs of the oil, and 1/2 tsp salt. Preheat the oven to 400°F. Line a baking sheet with parchment paper. On a lightly floured work surface, roll out the dough to a thin rectangle and transfer it to the baking sheet. Pierce the dough several times with a fork. Distribute the tomatoes over the dough. Clean the mushrooms and cut into very thin slices. Trim the fennel, wash, cut it into quarters, and then into thin slices. Distribute the mushrooms and fennel over the tomatoes. Season the pizza with salt, and sprinkle with the red pepper flakes and cheese. Drizzle the remaining 1/2 tbs oil over the top. Bake the pizza for 25–30 minutes on the middle oven shelf. Garnish with olives and basil, and serve.

Serves 2:

1/2 cup plain low-fat yogurt

1 cup all-purpose flour

1 tsp baking powder

3 tbs low-fat milk

2 1/2 tbs sunflower oil

Salt to taste

5 oz canned tomato pieces (drained)

3 oz mushrooms

1 small bulb fennel

1 tsp red pepper flakes

2 oz Gouda cheese, grated

6 black olives (pitted)

6–8 fresh basil leaves

➤ Chiles Spice up Your Figure

Eat something spicy and your brain will be flooded with endorphins, the messenger chemicals that ease pain and lift your spirits. A good mood translates into a more active and slender you. Spiciness also heats up the fat cells, causing them to be more likely to move.

POWER PER SERVING:

545 CALORIES

23 G PROTEIN • 23 G FAT

64 G CARBOHYDRATES

Bean Sprouts and Chicken Stir-Fry

Wok cooking preserves nutrients

Cut the chicken breast into thin strips and season with pepper. Rinse and drain the bean sprouts. Remove the stem, ribs and seeds from the bell pepper, and wash and cut it into strips. Trim the celery, wash, and cut it into thin slices. Peel the onion and dice it finely. In a small bowl, whisk together the chicken stock, soy sauce, sherry, and cornstarch in a bowl.

In a wok or skillet, heat 1 tbs of the oil over high heat. Stir-fry the chicken for about 3 minutes, then remove it from the pan. In the remaining oil, stir-fry the bell pepper, celery, and onion for 3 minutes. Add the sprouts and stir-fry for 1 minute.

Stir in the soy sauce mixture and stir-fry until the sauce thickens, about 2 minutes. Add the chicken, briefly heat through, and season with pepper. Sprinkle with cilantro and serve over the rice.

Serves 2:
7 oz boneless, skinless chicken breast
Black pepper to taste
7 oz bean sprouts
1 bell pepper
2 stalks celery
1 small onion
1/2 cup chicken stock
2 tbs soy sauce
2 tbs dry sherry
1 tsp cornstarch
1 1/2 tbs soybean oil
2 tbs chopped fresh cilantro
Cooked brown rice

POWER PER SERVING: 315 CALORIES • 37 G PROTEIN • 8 G FAT • 19 G CARBOHYDRATES

Spinach
A lighter version of a beloved classic
Saltimbocca

Serves 2:
10 oz fresh spinach
Salt to taste
Black pepper to taste
Freshly grated nutmeg to taste
4 thin chicken medallions
(about 2 oz each)
1 tbs olive oil
Juice of 1 lime
1/4 cup dry white wine
1/2 cup chicken stock
2 tsp cornstarch
Cooked whole-wheat fettuccine

Wash the spinach well and remove the stems. Blanch the spinach in boiling, salted water for 1 minute, plunge it into cold water and drain. Squeeze the moisture out of the spinach and chop it coarsely. Season with salt, pepper, and nutmeg.

Place 1 tbs of the spinach on top of each chicken medallion, fold them over, and fasten each one with a toothpick or wooden skewer. In a skillet, heat the oil over medium-high heat. Sauté the chicken medallions in the oil for 1–2 minutes on each side, remove them from the pan, and season with salt and pepper and keep warm. Mix together the lime juice, wine, stock and cornstarch, and add it to the skillet. Simmer over low heat until the mixture thickens. Season the sauce with salt and pepper. Add the chicken and the remaining spinach to the skillet and simmer, covered, for 2–3 minutes. Serve with the pasta.

White Meat

Meat is an important source of protein and iron, which makes it a fat burner. At the same time, however, beef, lamb, and pork contain a large amount of fat and purines. You should keep your consumption of red meat to a minimum. When you do indulge, choose the lower fat pieces from the fillet or tenderloin. Best of all, use white meat. Poultry and veal help you to go easy on bad fat.

POWER PER SERVING:

325 CALORIES

30 G PROTEIN • 14 G FAT

17 G CARBOHYDRATES

Sole with
Rich in iodine
Spring Vegetables

Season the sole fillets with salt and pepper, and spread each with 1/2 tbs of the crème fraîche. Wash and shake the tarragon dry, then remove the leaves from the stems. Sprinkle some of the tarragon leaves over the sole fillets and roll them up tightly.

Peel the kohlrabi and cut it into quarters. Peel the carrots. Cut both vegetables into thin slices. Trim and wash the sugar snap peas. Peel and dice the onion.

In a saucepan, heat the oil over medium heat. Add the onion and sauté until translucent. Add the kohlrabi, carrots and peas, and briefly sauté. Pour in the stock, cover the pan, and simmer the vegetables for 5 minutes. Season the vegetables with salt and pepper. Stir in the remaining crème fraîche. Place the rolled sole on top of the vegetables, cover, and simmer for 10 minutes over low heat. Chop the remaining tarragon and sprinkle on top. Serve with the rice

Serves 2:
4 sole fillets (about 2 oz each)
Salt to taste
White pepper to taste
1 1/2 tbs crème fraîche
1 sprig fresh tarragon
1 kohlrabi
7 oz baby carrots
5 oz sugar snap peas
1 small onion
1 tbs canola oil
2/3 cup vegetable stock
Cooked brown and wild rice

Fish, Please!

You should eat fish at least twice a week. It makes no difference what type—all fish is healthy. Salmon provides omega-3 fatty acids that prevent many chronic illnesses. Mackerel contains tyrosine, the material of fat-burning hormones. Fillet of sole is virtually fat-free.

POWER PER SERVING:

276 CALORIES

37 G PROTEIN • 13 G FAT

42 G CARBOHYDRATES

Stir-Fried Vegetables

Melt away fat with fish protein

with Shrimp

Trim and wash the sugar snap peas. Blanch the peas in boiling, salted water for 1 minute, plunge them into cold water, and drain. Remove the stem, ribs and seeds from the bell pepper, and wash and cut it into strips. Peel the shallot and finely chop.

In a skillet, heat the oil over medium heat. Add the peas, bell pepper and shallot, and sauté for 5 minutes. Season with salt and pepper.

Add the shrimp and sauté over low heat for 2 minutes. Cut the tomatoes in half and remove the stems. Wash the dill, shake dry, and chop. Add the tomato halves and dill to the skillet, and cook for an additional 2 minutes. Remove from the heat and toss with the lemon juice.

Serves 2:
5 oz sugar snap peas
Salt to taste
1 yellow bell pepper
1 shallot
1 tbs canola oil
Pepper to taste
5 oz raw peeled shrimp
4 oz cherry tomatoes
1/4 bunch fresh dill
1 tbs fresh lemon juice

▶ Midnight Snacks

Just before going to bed, raid the refrigerator one last time. For efficient fat burning you'll need protein and carbohydrates. Half a serving of yogurt with 2 tbs of oat flakes stimulates the hormone serotonin for a peaceful sleep as well as growth hormone, which breaks down fat and builds up muscle while you quietly slumber.

POWER PER SERVING:

161 CALORIES

33 G PROTEIN • 5 G FAT

43 G CARBOHYDRATES

Monkfish Ragout

Fill up your tank with "super"

with Lentils

Wash and peel the potatoes and carrot, then dice them. Trim the leek, slit it open lengthwise, and wash and cut it into rings. Peel and dice the onion.

Serves 2:
5 oz firm potatoes
1 carrot
1 small leek
1 small onion
2 tsp olive oil
1 cup vegetable stock
7 oz cooked brown lentils
1/2 cup organic tomato sauce
Salt to taste
Black pepper to taste
10 oz monkfish fillet
2 tsp lemon juice
2 tbs chopped fresh Italian parsley

In a wide saucepan, heat the oil over medium heat and sauté the onion in it until translucent. Add the potatoes, carrot and leek, and sauté for 3 minutes. Pour in the stock, cover, and simmer for 10 minutes over low heat.

Add the lentils, tomato sauce, salt, and pepper. Simmer the mixture for an additional 3 minutes over medium heat.

Cut the fish into cubes, and season it with the lemon juice, salt, and pepper. Add the fish to the pan, cover, and simmer for 3–4 minutes over low heat. Season to taste with salt and pepper. Sprinkle parsley over the top.

Olive Oil

Olive oil is the fountain of youth in Mediterranean countries. You too can cook with this precious tonic for a healthy heart and a slender figure. And don't skimp on the quality. Go for the purest and most natural "extra virgin" oil.

POWER PER SERVING:

565 CALORIES

49 G PROTEIN • 9 G FAT

70 G CARBOHYDRATES

Tuna Skewers

Feast and stay thin

with Saffron Rice

Peel the onion and dice it finely. In a saucepan, heat 1 tbs of the oil over medium heat and briefly sauté the onion in it. Add the saffron and the rice, and sauté for 2 minutes. Pour in the wine and let it simmer. Heat the stock, stir it into the rice, cover the pan, and cook for 40 minutes over low heat.

Cut the tuna into 1/2 inch cubes. Peel the onion and cut it into eighths. Remove the stem, ribs and seeds from the pepper, and wash and cut it into pieces. Wash and trim the zucchini and cut into thick slices. Rinse and shake dry the sage. Alternately thread pieces of fish, onion, bell pepper, zucchini, and sage onto wooden skewers. Peel and mince the garlic, and mix it with the lemon juice, salt, and pepper in a shallow dish. Add the tuna skewers to the dish, coat the ingredients with the marinade, and set aside for about 30 minutes.

In a skillet, heat the remaining 1 tbs oil over medium heat. Sauté the skewers for 12–15 minutes, turning occasionally. Season the saffron rice with salt and pepper, and serve with the tuna skewers.

Serves 2:

1 small red onion

2 tbs olive oil

2 pinches powdered saffron

3/4 cup short-grain brown rice

1/4 cup dry white wine

1 1/4 cups vegetable stock

5 oz tuna fillet

1 small white onion

1 small yellow bell pepper

4 oz zucchini

8 fresh sage leaves

1 small clove garlic

1 tbs lemon juice

Salt to taste

Black pepper to taste

POWER PER SERVING: 570 CALORIES • 18 G PROTEIN • 25 G FAT • 63 G CARBOHYDRATES

Beauty Food

Beauty
Strengthen and care for your skin and body—from the inside
from Within

EAT YOUR WAY TO HEALTH AND BEAUTY

Beauty is more than simply having a good figure. Vitality and good health play an important part. Skin, hair, and nails are fortified by various vitamins and minerals that must come from the food we eat. Our digestive system releases them from what we consume, and our blood circulation transports them to where they are used. At the same time, the blood absorbs waste materials, carries them to the liver and kidneys for detoxification, and expels them. This process is essential, since our cells are constantly renewing themselves. The more smoothly this process of removal and renewal runs, the more beautiful you will become.

BUILDING BLOCKS OF NUTRITION

First of all, the food we eat is converted into energy, which is measured in kilocalories (commonly shortened into calories). The body "burns" this energy during metabolism, or uses parts of it as building blocks to regenerate itself.

These building blocks are:

* Carbohydrates, which are the principal component of fruit, vegetables, and grains. Carbohydrate-rich foods also provide fiber, water-soluble vitamins, and minerals. However, some carbohydrates also contain fast-releasing sugar, which, if eaten in excess, can make us tired and lethargic.
* Protein, which is considered a building block of our body's cells. It is present in enzymes, hormones, and antibodies, and carries our genetic materials. Protein is needed constantly for proper cell renewal. It is found in fish, meat, eggs, dairy products, cereals, and grains.

* Fat, which is a component of hormones and bile acids. It carries fat-soluble vitamins, and is a component of cell walls—and thus of our skin. Unsaturated fatty acids are vital to health, and are contained in good-quality, cold-pressed oils. The hidden fats in foods like meat products, cakes and cookies, though delicious, are tricky, and can contribute to the storage of excess fat deposits.

* Fiber, a substance that can help banish sluggishness. It consists of plant cellulose, which your body doesn't digest, so it contains no calories. Fiber is present mainly in fruit, vegetables, and grains. It ensures that waste products are quickly expelled from the body. Fiber also fills us up without leading to weight gain.

THE LITTLE THINGS THAT MEAN A LOT

The body is unable to produce a lot of the active substances that monitor and control our metabolism; we need to absorb them from the food we eat. And although we need only the tiniest quantities of these substances, we often do not get enough of them. You can read more about this on the chart on the next pages.

* Minerals are the building blocks for bones, teeth, hair, and blood—but they also regulate the central metabolic processes, and maintain our inner balance.
* Vitamins are involved in all metabolic processes, and play a decisive role in processing foods in our diet; in other words, they help us to produce energy. Vitamins strengthen our immune system, regulate our mineral balance, and control cell regulation.
* Although so-called "bioactive" substances (phytochemicals, or plant chemicals) are not essential, they do play a key role in keeping us healthy and feeling good. They are created during the metabolic process of plants, so they are present in fruit, vegetables, and grains. Many bioactive substances not only help prevent circulatory problems and atherosclerosis (clogging of the arteries), but also protect the cells against environmental damage.

Nutrient	Effect
Vitamin D	Prevents osteoporosis by stimulating the body to absorb more calcium
Vitamin E	Antioxidant–protects against free radicals; keeps tissues elastic, stimulates the circulation
Vitamin B_1	Strengthens nerves and muscles
Vitamin B_2	Aids in protein metabolism, cell division, nervous system; combats PMS and morning sickness
Vitamin B_{12}	Essential for cell division and blood formation
Niacin	Promotes smooth skin and calm nerves; aids in energy utilization
Pantothenic acid	Promotes skin and hair renewal; aids healing
Folic acid	Promotes cell division and formation, formation of blood cells, immune system health
Iron	Aids in formation of blood cells, healthy skin, shiny hair, strong fingernails
Selenium	Contributes to healthy skin and nails; aids in detoxification
Zinc	Promotes strong hair and healthy skin; aids healing and the immune system; improves sensuality
Iodine	Contributes to proper function of metabolism; helps maintain a slim figure
Calcium	Forms strong bones, teeth, nails, and hair; benefits the nerves
Silicic acid	Firms tissues; strengthens skin and hair
Lactic acid	Beneficial to intestinal flora and the immune system; aids iron absorption
Omega-3-fatty acids	Aids circulation; helps maintain a healthy heart
Gamma-linoleic acid	Contributes to healthy, firm skin
Carotenoids	Boost the immune system; beta-carotene, a precursor of vitamin A, contributes to smooth, healthy skin

Found In

Oily fish, egg yolks, butter. Produced by the skin when exposed to sun

High-quality plant oils, especially wheat germ oil, fish, grains, and nuts

Whole wheat products, yeast, potatoes

Whole wheat products, fish, shellfish, cabbage, leeks, beans

Meat, fish, dairy products, foods containing lactic acid, yeast extract

Whole wheat products, meat, fish, potatoes

Liver, yeast, mushrooms, whole wheat products

Raw green vegetables, nuts, seeds, yeast, oranges, mangos

Meat, fish, millet, green vegetables, dried fruit, nuts

Fish (especially tuna and herring), whole grains, vegetables, mushrooms

Brewer's yeast, cheese, liver, nuts, sea vegetables, oysters

Shellfish, iodized salt, sea vegetables

Milk, yogurt, cottage cheese, tofu, collard greens

Whole grains, especially millet, oats, barley

Sauerkraut, pickled gherkins, yogurt, kefir, buttermilk, cheese, salami, olives, soy sauce

Oily fish (herring, salmon), flaxseed and canola oils

Plant oils (borage, sunflower, thistle, flaxseed), avocados, fish

Yellow, red, and green fruits and vegetables, such as apricots, winter squash, and broccoli

Beauty
everything for beauty
Basics

THE AMAZING POWERS OF NATURAL OILS

Though recent thinking has ruled fats unfavorable, we actually need them to stay alive. Plant oils contain many fats that are beneficial to our health and appearance. Cold-pressed plant oils retain more of sensitive substances and delicate aromas than heat processed oils. The following oils are especially beneficial:

✳ Black cumin oil*—contains polyunsaturated fatty acids and minerals that are effective against allergic and inflammatory symptoms. The oil has a spicy, Asian aroma.

✳ Borage oil*—contains a good amount of gamma linoleic acid, which is effective against eczema and general skin irritations. Use in moderation.

✳ Canola oil—also contains plenty of omega-3 fatty acids, and has a fresh flavor; a good choice for salad dressings and stir-fries.

✳ Flaxseed oil*—contains good amounts of omega-3 fatty acids. It's yellow in color, has a slightly bitter aroma, and goes well with strong flavors.

✳ Olive oil—consists mainly of monounsaturated fatty acids that prevent the arteries from clogging.

✳ Wheat germ oil*—contains an exceptionally high proportion of vitamin E, has a grainy-nutty flavor, and goes well in sweet dishes.

The oils listed above can be found in supermarkets or health-food stores, or from mail-order sources. Many are available from Internet suppliers.

*Store these valuable oils in the refrigerator, and use them within a few days. Bring them to room temperature and mix well before using.

WATER FOR FIRMNESS

Our bodies consist of at least two-thirds water, the amount of which decreases as we age. Water dissolves and transports the water-soluble nutrients in our body. It regulates the body's temperature and removes hazardous materials. Water makes the skin firm and smooth. For maximum benefit, our bodies need between 1.5 and 2 quarts of water a day—more in warm weather or if we are performing hard physical work or vigorous exercise.

Fresh from the Sea

Sea water contains lots of minerals, some of which are rare on dry land, such as iodine, iron, calcium, magnesium, fluoride, and zinc. Sea vegetables, mussels, oysters, and crustaceans filter these minerals out of the sea, and concentrate them.

❀ Nori (dried seaweed) is available roasted and formed into fine sheets. Nori is commonly used to make sushi. It is delicate, slightly spicy, high in protein, contains large amounts of vitamins A and C, and plenty of calcium and iron. Look for nori in a well-stocked supermarket or Japanese market.

❀ Sea vegetables provide many beneficial nutrients. Arame is a brown sea vegetable that is bursting with iodine and calcium. Arame contains more iron and vitamin B_{12} than meat, and is therefore ideal for a meat-free diet. Dulse is a type of red seaweed with many of the same qualities as arame. Before cooking, sea vegetables should be soaked in water for about 5 minutes, until they double in volume. Sea vegetables can be found in health food stores or Asian markets.

❀ Oily saltwater fish, such as salmon, tuna, mackerel, and herring, contain large amounts of highly beneficial omega-3 fatty acids. They also contain good quantities of protein and iodine.

❀ Shrimp, mussels, and oysters, are delicate reserves of zinc, iron, selenium, and fluoride.

Natural
for healthy-looking skin and shiny hair
Skincare

BALSAM FOR THE SKIN

Our skin breathes through the pores, where it eliminates waste products and absorbs beneficial substances. Cold-pressed oils, fruit, vegetables, milk, and other dairy products contain substances that effect the skin in a number of different ways. Below, find several masks made from fresh, natural ingredients, based on skin type. After mixing, apply to the face and neck, then cover with a moist cloth and relax for 20-30 minutes. The benefits are even greater if you can lie down and relax while the mask works. Rinse off the mask with plenty of lukewarm water, and apply a nourishing cream. These masks are gentle and can be safely applied once or twice a week.

PEACH MASK: FOR ANY SKIN TYPE

For best results, choose a ripe, fragrant peach. Peel and chop the peach, then mash with a fork.

AVOCADO MASK: FOR DRY SKIN

Peel 1 ripe avocado, and puree with a few drops of lemon juice and 1 teaspoon of borage oil.

CUCUMBER OR SAUERKRAUT MASK: FOR OILY SKIN

Wash and peel the cucumber, then grate it. Refreshes and smoothes the skin. You could also use freshly prepared sauerkraut (from a delicatessen), which is astringent and anti-inflammatory.

COTTAGE CHEESE MASK: FOR TIRED SKIN

Drain 3 tablespoons of low-fat cottage cheese, and combine with 1 tablespoon lemon juice, 1 tablespoon buttermilk, and 1 teaspoon wheat germ oil, stirring until the mixture is smooth.

SKINCARE FOR THE BODY

If you would like to do something to benefit the skin on your whole body, a combination of massage and bath is ideal. The temperature of the bath water should be between 98.6°F (body temperature) and 102°F. Do not spend more than 15-20 minutes in the tub. A bath that's too long and too hot will dry the skin rather than care for it.

While you are in the bath, soak a washcloth in the bath water and place it on your face. Do this several times. This opens the pores and helps to cleanse the skin. Good tip: after your bath, apply one of the beauty masks above and relax on the bed or couch for half an hour. Incidentally, cold-pressed oils, especially wheat germ, sesame, and olive oil, are wonderful for the skin—and contain no additives. Borage oil is especially good for dry, irritable skin.

TREAT FOR DRY SKIN
Before bathing, massage your whole body, from top to toe, with wheat germ oil, working from the extremities toward the heart. Then run your bath, adding 3 quarts of buttermilk or milk.

PURIFY OILY SKIN
Stand in the shower and massage your body with wheat bran. Then, pour 2 cups of fruit vinegar into the bath water.

NOURISH YOUR HAIR
Your hair is nourished from the roots. Central heating, sun, and cold air are bad for the hair, turning it dry and brittle. Apply a strengthening pack from time to time—it works like magic. Wash your hair as you normally would, then apply the lukewarm pack to your hair, avoiding your scalp but paying particular attention to the roots. Then, put on a shower cap, wrap a towel around your head to keep it warm, and let the pack do its work for at least 1 hour. Afterwards, wash your hair thoroughly with a mild shampoo.

HERB AND OIL PACK
Pour 1 1/4 cups of cold-pressed olive oil over 2-3 sprigs of fresh thyme, 1 sprig of fresh rosemary, and 1/2 handful of birch leaves (from a personal care or beauty supply store). Place the concoction in a cool, dark place for 1-4 weeks. Pass the oil through a strainer and squeeze out the herbs. Measure out the amount you need to cover your head before applying, then heat slightly.

EGG AND OIL PACK
Depending on the length of your hair, beat 1-2 egg yolks with 1-2 teaspoons of cold-pressed wheat germ oil. Heat the mixture until lukewarm and rub into your hair.

Power

well-being and relaxation at home

Week

SPOIL YOURSELF!

You don't have the time or money for a week at a spa? Then spoil yourself at home using the recipes in this book. Do something for your body at the same time—go swimming, cycling, or jogging. Spend 15 minutes a day doing some exercise. And, as a special indulgence, treat yourself to a visit to the beauty salon. A massage followed by a steam bath or sauna will also do you good.

MINI SPA

Of course, you can't expect miracles in just a week, but it can be a new beginning.
In corporate some of the things you do in this week into your everyday life: drink lots of water, eat lots of fruit and vegetables, use a minimum of fat in your cooking—but make sure you do not miss out on the valuable fats. You will find that this short "cure" is a culinary delight. You will not be hungry: you can eat as many raw vegetables and berries, apples, and citrus fruit as you like for the duration of the week. But take care not to spend the whole day "grazing"—have three good meals a day, and maybe a snack in the morning or afternoon.

DRINK YOURSELF BEAUTIFUL

Drink as much herbal and green tea as you like. For best results, you can drink about two cups of ordinary tea and coffee per day, adding a little low-fat milk and cane sugar or honey—if you need it! Or, drink sparkling water, adding a splash of apple or lemon juice if desired. And what about alcohol? Well, it's bad news for your looks, but it can definitely add to a celebratory mood. For example, you can have a glass of dry Champagne to kick off your Power Week. But spare yourself on Sunday: make sure you get lots of sleep, go for a swim and a sauna, have a soak, and put a mask on your skin and a pack on your hair to motivate yourself for the week. That's not to say you must follow our suggestions to the letter: have a bowl of low-fat granola and a drink in the morning, then one cold and one hot main meal of your choice later in the day.

EATING PLAN FOR THE WEEK

Monday

- Buckwheat and Apple Granola
- Cabbage and Apple Salad
- Spicy Beef Stir-Fry with Avocado; 1 slice of whole wheat bread

Tuesday

- Mocha Milkshake; 1 slice of whole wheat bread
- Green Bean and Shrimp Salad; 1 slice of whole wheat bread
- Turkey Breast with Endive

Wednesday

- Citrus Muesli, Apple Cooler
- Choco-Risotto
- Boiled Potatoes with Creamy Power Spread

Thursday

- Melon Puree with Fruited Risotto; Orange-Scented Barley Water
- Dry-Cured Beef Sandwich
- Green Veggie Ragout

Friday

- Orange and Carrot Cottage Cheese
- Pesto-Mozzarella Sandwich
- Millet Spaghetti with Carrots

Saturday

- Six-Grain Granola with Fruit
- Fruited Cottage Cheese
- Chinese Fondue; Grapefruit and Carrot Salad

Sunday

- Fruit Salad with Grapes; Avocado-Fruit Drink
- Lime-Marinated Ceviche; fruit of your choice
- Artichokes with Avocado Dip; Lamb Cutlets with Vegetables

Avocado

light and creamy for

Fruit

a little extra energy

Drink

Serves 2: 1 small, soft avocado • 2 sprigs fresh lemon balm or mint • 1/4 cup fresh lemon juice • 1 1/4 cups pear juice • 1 tsp borage oil

Halve the avocado, remove the pit, and scrape out the flesh with a spoon. Wash and shake dry the lemon balm or mint, and remove the leaves from the stalks. In a blender, puree the avocado, lemon balm or mint leaves, lemon juice, pear juice, and borage oil. Dilute to taste with ice-cold water.

power

PER PORTION: 205 calories • 2 g protein • 13 g fat • 24 g carbohydrates

Orange-Scented

lifts the mood and counters water retention

Barley Water

Serves 2: 2 oz pearl barley • 1 1/2 quarts water • Juice of 1 orange

Rinse the barley well. Place it in a saucepan with the water and bring to a boil. Reduce the heat, cover tightly, and simmer for 30 minutes. Strain, saving the cooking liquid, and reserving the barley for another use. Let the liquid cool, then place it in the refrigerator until chilled. Combine the barley water with the fruit juice, and drink well chilled.

PER DRINK: 120 calories • 4 g protein • 1 g fat • 24 g carbohydrates

Mocha

detoxifies and aids digestion

Milkshake

Serves 2: 2 1/2 cups acidopholous milk • 1 tbs instant espresso • 1 tsp cocoa powder • 1 tsp bee pollen • 1 tbs oats • 2-3 tbs honey • 1 small banana (optional)

Combine the milk, espresso, cocoa powder, pollen, oats, and honey in a blender. Blend until the ingredients are smooth and dissolved. For a milder flavor and additional nutrients, blend in the banana.

PER DRINK: 85 calories • 3 g protein • 0 g fat • 19 g carbohydrates

Apple
cleanses from within
Cooler

Serves 2: 1 1/4 cups apple juice • 1 1/4 cups sparkling water • 1/4 cup cider vinegar

• 1 tbs honey • 1 tsp bee pollen

Combine the apple juice, water, vinegar, honey, and bee pollen. Mix the ingredients well until everything is dissolved. It's best to sip this at room temperature.

power

PER DRINK: 100 calories • 0 g protein • 0 g fat • 26 g carbohydrates

Orange-Aloe
with lots of vitamin C and beta-carotene
Cooler

Serves 2: 6 tbs aloe vera juice • 1 1/2 cups freshly squeezed orange juice • 1 tsp

borage oil • 1 tbs wheat germ

In a blender, combine the aloe vera juice, orange juice, oil, and wheat germ. Blend well at the highest speed, then pour into tall glasses and serve immediately.

power

PER DRINK: 137 calories • 3 g protein • 3 g fat • 26 g carbohydrates

Citus
stimulating and skin friendly
Muesli

Peel the grapefruit or oranges with a sharp knife, removing the white pith.

Slice the grapefruit or oranges into quarters, and remove the white

Serves 2:

1 pink grapefruit, or 2 oranges

1 small or 1/4 large fresh
ripe pineapple

2 oz flaked millet

2 tbs wheat germ

1 tbs bee pollen

1/2 cup multivitamin juice

membrane from the middle. Cut the quarters into
slices, collecting the juice.

Peel the pineapple, remove the brown "eyes," cut
it lengthwise into quarters, and remove the core.
Cut into bite-sized pieces, collecting the juice.
Place the chopped fruit and juice, flaked millet,
wheat germ, bee pollen, and multivitamin juice in
a bowl, and mix. Divide the muesli among two
dishes and serve.

Pineapple

Fresh pineapple contains large
amounts of the enzyme *bromelin*,
which breaks down protein. It is
diuretic, sudorific, and cleanses
the skin.

PER PORTION:

205 calories

5 g protein

2 g fat

42 g carbohydrates

Six-Grain Granola

with bioactive bee pollen

with Fruit

Serves 2: 8 dried apricots • 8 dried plums • 2 oz six-grain cereal • 2 1/2 cups acidopholous milk • 2 tbs honey • 2 tbs sesame seeds • 1 tsp bee pollen

Rinse the apricots and plums, and cut them into small pieces. Bring the cereal, dried fruit, and 1 1/2 cups of the milk to a boil in a saucepan. Remove from the heat, and stir in the honey and remaining 1 cup milk. Let the mixture cool. Stir in the sesame seeds and the bee pollen, and serve.

PER PORTION: 405 calories • 8 g protein • 4 g fat • 87 g carbohydrates

Buckwheat and

with lots of oats and yogurt

Apple Granola

Serves 2: 2 oz buckwheat groats • 2 apples • 2 tbs oat bran • 5 tbs oat flakes • 2 cups plain yogurt • 1 tsp borage oil • 3-4 tbs maple syrup

Toast the buckwheat in a dry nonstick skillet over medium heat, until you begin to smell it. Wash and dry the apples, then grate them coarsely (do not peel). Mix the grated apples with the oat bran, oat flakes, toasted buckwheat, yogurt, borage oil, and maple syrup. Divide among 2 bowls, and serve.

PER PORTION: 490 calories • 14 g protein • 13 g fat • 81 g carbohydrates

Fruited

with protein-rich Special K

Cottage Cheese

Place the cottage cheese in a bowl. Add the orange juice and beat well for a few minutes with a mixer. Add the yeast flakes and wheat germ, and stir until smooth.

Wash and peel the carrot, then grate it coarsely. Stir the grated carrot into the cottage cheese mixture. Chop the melon and stir it into the mixture. Stir in the Special K or other cereal. Spoon the mixture into bowls and serve immediately.

Serves 2:

8 oz low-fat cottage cheese

1/2 cup orange juice

1 tbs yeast flakes

1 tbs wheat germ

1 baby carrot

10 oz melon (peeled)

6-8 tbs Special K cereal, or any other low-sugar, crunchy cereal, such as corn flakes

Power pack for the skin

Everything you eat affects your appearance. Wheat germ contains vitamins E, B_1, B_6, and folic acid, as well as magnesium, iron, and zinc. Raw grains contain a substance called *phytin*, which hinders mineral absorption; to prevent this, grains should be first soaked and boiled. Bee pollen contains concentrated nutrients, enzymes, and bioactive substances. Yogurt contains active bacteria which helps the digestive system.

PER PORTION:

270 calories

25 g protein

4 g fat

35 g carbohydrates

Lime-Marinated
Ceviche
with tomatoes, ginger, and fresh herbs

To make the marinade, mix together the lime juice and vinegar in a wide, shallow bowl. Wash the fish and pat dry with paper towels. Cut it into small pieces. Place the fish in the marinade, turning occasionally.

Wash and halve the tomatoes, remove the stalks and cores, and dice. Set the tomatoes aside, but transfer any seeds and juice that have escaped to the bowl with the fish. Peel the onion and slice thinly. Wash the herbs and shake dry. Remove the herb leaves from the stalks, and chop them finely. Peel and finely chop the ginger.

Spread the onion slices over a plate, followed by the diced tomato and the fish; sprinkle with the herbs. Sprinkle each layer with a little salt, pepper, marinade, and oil, and top with the chopped ginger. Serve with the bread.

Serves 2:
Juice of 1 lime
2 tbs cider vinegar
7 oz fish fillets, such as snapper or sole
2 large, ripe tomatoes
1 small sweet onion
1 bunch fresh cilantro or Italian parsley
Walnut-sized piece fresh ginger
Sea salt to taste
Black pepper to taste
1 tsp black cumin oil
Thinly sliced bread for accompaniment

Bounty from the sea

The more natural the state of the fish and vegetables you eat, the better they are for you. Don't discard the tomato seeds—they provide fiber, and cleanse your body from within. Tomatoes' best nutrients are right below the skin. Fish "cooked" in citrus juice instead of over heat retains its natural iodine and omega-3 fatty acids.

PER PORTION:
150 calories
19 g protein
5 g fat
8 g carbohydrates

Asparagus and
with spicy nori
Mushroom Salad

Serves 2:
6 tbs cider vinegar
1 tbs freshly grated
horseradish
2 tbs canola oil
2 tbs soy sauce
Black pepper to taste
6 tbs water or white wine
10 oz thick asparagus
4 oz large mushrooms
2 sheets nori
1 tbs sesame seeds
Sourdough rye bread for
accompaniment

To make the dressing, stir together the vinegar, horseradish, oil, soy sauce, pepper, and water or wine. Wash and trim the asparagus. Carefully peel the lower third of the stalks, then slice thinly. Trim the mushrooms, rinse quickly, and cut into thin slices. Cut the nori sheets into 11/2-inch pieces. Line 2 large plates with half of the nori, and drizzle with a little of the dressing. Divide the sliced asparagus, mushrooms, and the remaining nori among the plates, then drizzle with the remaining dressing. Toast the sesame seeds in a dry nonstick skillet, tossing occasionally, until you begin to smell them, and sprinkle over the salad. Let the salad stand for 30 minutes, then serve with the bread.

Horseradish

Horseradish contains mustard oil, which has natural antibiotic properties that support stomach acid. It also stimulates the digestive juices. Horseradish contains even more vitamin C than red bell peppers.

PER PORTION:

160 calories

5 g protein

10 g fat

8 g carbohydrates

power

Roast Beef
with arugula and pumpkin seeds
Carpaccio

To make the dressing, place the pumpkin seed and wheat germ oils, orange juice, salt, pepper, and mustard in a bowl, and whisk well. Thoroughly wash the arugula, pick over, and drain well.

Divide half of the arugula among 2 plates, and drizzle with a little of the dressing. Then, arrange the roast beef and remaining arugula leaves on top, and drizzle with the remaining dressing.

Coarsely chop the pumpkin seeds and sprinkle over the salad. Let the ingredients stand for about 30 minutes to blend the flavors. Serve with the bread.

Serves 2:

2 tbs pumpkin seed oil

1 tbs wheat germ oil

1/2 cup orange juice

Sea salt to taste

Black pepper to taste

1 tsp dry mustard

4 oz arugula

6 oz rare roast beef, very thinly sliced

2 tbs pumpkin seeds

Ciabatta or baguette for accompaniment

Dry mustard

Made of ground mustard seeds, dry mustard adds a gentle spiciness to salad dressings and marinades without adding acidity. Mustard aids digestion, is antibacterial, and promotes blood flow to the body's tissues. It is also good for indigestion. You can use prepared mustard as a substitute.

PER PORTION:

340 calories

23 g protein

23 g fat

11 g carbohydrates

Artichokes with
with basil and black cumin oil
Avocado Dip

Wash the artichokes. Break off the stalks, remove the outer leaves, and cut off any sharp tips. Bring the water to a boil with the sugar and vinegar.

Serves 2:
2 large artichokes
2 cups water
Pinch of sugar
Dash of cider vinegar
1 bunch fresh basil
1 ripe avocado
2 tbs fresh lemon juice
1 tsp black cumin oil
Sea salt to taste
White pepper to taste

Cook the artichokes in the boiling water for about 30 minutes, until you can easily pull out a leaf. Remove the artichokes and reserve the cooking liquid. Wash and shake dry the basil, and remove the leaves from the stalks. Halve the avocado, and remove the pit. In a blender, puree the avocado flesh with a little of the artichoke cooking liquid and the lemon juice. Stir in the oil. Season the dip with salt and pepper, and serve as an accompaniment to the warm or cooled artichokes.

Versatile artichokes

Artichokes contain a substance called *cynarine*, which stimulates the liver and thereby cleanses the blood. It also encourages cell renewal, which makes the skin radiant. Beta-carotene and vitamin E aid this effect. You can add honey to the cooking liquid, then refrigerate it and serve as an unusual apéritif.

PER PORTION:
180 calories
5 g protein
14 g fat
11 g carbohydrates

power

Grapefruit and Carrot Salad

with red lentils and sea vegetables

Serves 2:

2 tbs arame or dulse
1 1/2 cups water
3/4 cup red lentils
Sea salt to taste
1 tsp powdered ginger
7 oz baby carrots
7 oz spinach
1 small onion
1 pink grapefruit
3 tbs wheat germ oil
1 tsp dry mustard
Black pepper to taste
Hot cooked rice for accompaniment

In a saucepan, soak the arame or dulse in the water for 5 minutes. Add the red lentils, salt, and ginger. Cover tightly and simmer over low heat for 10 minutes; remove from the heat to prevent the sea vegetables from absorbing too much liquid. Meanwhile, wash and peel the carrots, and grate them coarsely. Wash and pick over the spinach, remove any coarse stalks, and cut the leaves into strips. Peel and finely chop the onion. Halve the grapefruit and use a spoon to scoop out segments of the flesh. Squeeze the juice from the grapefruit halves. Add the juice, grapefruit pieces, wheat germ oil, and dry mustard to the lentil and sea vegetables mixture, and carefully stir in the grated carrot and spinach strips. Season well with salt and pepper, and serve warm, accompanied by the rice.

Grapefruit

Just one grapefruit provides an adult's daily vitamin C requirement. It also stimulates the circulatory system, contributing to skin radiance.

PER PORTION:

440 calories

22 g protein

17 g fat

51 g carbohydrates

Broccoli and
with lots of vitamin E
Sauerkraut Salad

Wash the broccoli florets and drain in a strainer. Chop them a little, then puree in a blender, adding a little water to achieve a smooth texture. Drain the corn in the strainer. Coarsely chop the sauerkraut with a knife, then add it to a bowl with the corn and pureed broccoli, mixing well. Coarsely chop the sunflower kernels. Peel and finely chop the garlic.

To make the dressing, place the sunflower kernels, garlic, yogurt, oil, and vinegar in a bowl, and mix well. Season with the salt, pepper, thyme, and ginger. Pour the dressing over the vegetables and toss well. Arrange the salad on plates, and serve with bread or potatoes.

Serves 2:
5 oz broccoli florets
1-2 tbs water
1 can sweet corn kernels (7 oz)
8 oz sauerkraut (drained)
2 tbs sunflower kernels
1 clove garlic
2/3 cup plain yogurt
2 tbs nut oil
1-2 tbs cider vinegar
Sea salt to taste
Black pepper to taste
1 tsp fresh thyme leaves
1/2 tsp powdered ginger
Crusty bread or boiled small
potatoes for accompaniment

Sauerkraut

Sauerkraut contains lactic acid, potassium, calcium, and iodine, as well as vitamin C. It aids digestion, and strengthens tissues. Fresh sauerkraut (non-canned) from a delicatessen is especially effective for enhancing beauty.

PER PORTION:

355 calories

11 g protein

23 g fat

31 g carbohydrates

power

Melon Puree
and fresh berries
with Fruited Risotto

Heat the oil in a pan over low heat. Add the rice and the pine nuts, and gently sauté until the rice becomes slightly translucent. Pour in half of the juice and simmer gently, stirring continuously, until the rice texture starts to become grainy. Add the remaining juice, and bring to a boil again briefly. Remove the pan from the heat, cover tightly, and let stand until cool. Refrigerate the mixture until ready to serve, up to overnight.

Cut the melon into chunks. In a blender, puree the melon flesh with the honey. Wash the berries and cut into bite-sized pieces, if necessary. Pour the melon puree into deep bowls and stir in the berries, dividing evenly. Top each serving with a scoop of the rice and serve.

Serves 2:

1 tsp wheat germ oil

1/2 cup Arborio rice

2 tbs pine nuts

1 1/2 cups apple, orange, or grape juice

12 oz cantaloupe (peeled)

1 tbs honey

1 cup fresh seasonal berries

Multi-vitamin fruit juices
Some fruit juices contain added vitamins, such as A, C, and E. The primary function of these health-promoting beverages is cell protection.

PER PORTION:

425 calories

7 g protein

6 g fat

84 g carbohydrates

power

Fruit Salad
and toasted buckwheat
with Grapes

Serves 2: 7 oz seedless grapes • 1 apple • 1 orange • 2 tbs raisins • 1/2 cup apple, orange, or grape juice • 2 oz buckwheat groats • 2 tbs sesame seeds

Wash the fruit. Remove the grapes from the stalks. Cut the apple into eighths, remove the core, and cut each piece in half. Peel the orange, divide into segments, and cut into thirds. Place the fruit in a bowl with the raisins and juice. Toast the buckwheat and sesame seeds in a dry nonstick skillet, tossing occasionally, until you begin to smell them. Cool slightly, then sprinkle over the fruit.

PER PORTION: 295 calories • 6 g protein • 5 g fat • 60 g carbohydrates

Orange and Carrot
with high-vitamin-C rosehip extract
Cottage Cheese

Serves 2: 2 small carrots • 1 orange • 1 tbs rosehip extract • 1-2 tbs honey • 8 oz low-fat cottage cheese • 1 tsp bee pollen • 1 oz sliced almonds

Wash, peel, and finely grate the carrots. Peel the orange and cut into slices, then cut each slice into eighths. In a bowl, mix the rosehip extract with the honey, then gradually add the cottage cheese and bee pollen, mixing well. Stir in the grated carrot, orange pieces with juice, and the almonds.

PER PORTION: 200 calories • 17 g protein • 6 g fat • 20 g carbohydrates

Choco-
with dried dates
Risotto

Rinse the dates and chop into small pieces. Place the rice in a saucepan and warm gently over low heat, then pour in the milk. Add the chopped dates, cocoa powder, and honey.

Cover tightly and simmer gently over low heat for about 50 minutes, stirring occasionally, until the liquid has been absorbed. Remove the pan from the heat and let the rice cool completely.

Beat the cream until stiff peaks form. Gently mix it with the rice and serve immediately.

Serves 2:
4 oz pitted dried dates
3/4 cup Arborio rice
2 1/2 cups low-fat milk
1 tbs cocoa powder
1-2 tbs honey
1/2 cup heavy cream

Dates
These dried fruits contain good amounts of iron and potassium. Because they are naturally sweet, they are an ideal substitute for sugar. Dates are also high in fiber, which gently stimulates digestion.

PER PORTION:

560 calories

10 g protein

18 g fat

87 g carbohydrates

Green Bean and

with vitamin-packed sea vegetables

Shrimp Salad

Serves 2:

2 tbs arame or dulse

1 1/2 cups water

10 oz fresh green beans

1 small onion

1 tbs olive oil

Sea salt to taste

Black pepper to taste

1 tsp fresh thyme leaves

7 oz tomatoes

10 black olives (pitted)

7 oz small peeled cooked shrimp

2–3 tbs cider vinegar

Soak the arame or dulse in the water for 5 minutes. Meanwhile, wash and trim the beans, and remove any strings. Peel, halve, and finely chop the onion. In a skillet, heat the oil over medium heat. Add the onion and beans and sauté until the onion is translucent. Add the arame or dulse with the soaking water, and season the vegetables with salt and pepper. Add the thyme and simmer everything gently for about 15 minutes, until the beans are tender-crisp. Let the mixture cool.

Wash the tomatoes, remove the cores, and cut them into thin wedges. Cut the olives into thin slices. Drain the shrimp, if necessary, and add to the bean mixture along with the tomatoes and olives. Stir in the cider vinegar to taste.

Olives & olive oil – a healthy duo

Olives are good for the circulation, and stabilize blood pressure. They contain lactic acid, which is full of unsaturated fatty acids. Another beauty-enhancing substance in olive products is *squalene*, which keeps the skin healthy and smooth, and stimulates the immune system.

PER PORTION:

225 calories

23 g protein

9 g fat

14 g carbohydrates

Cabbage and

with fresh dill and walnuts

Apple Salad

Wash the cabbage and apples. Cut the cabbage into quarters, remove the core, and finely slice the cabbage pieces. Dry the apples and grate them coarsely without peeling them. In a bowl, mix together the sliced cabbage and grated apple. Stir the sauerkraut juice and lemon juice into the apple and cabbage mixture. Season well with salt and pepper. Let the mixture stand for about 1 hour to develop the flavors.

Serves 2:

7 oz white cabbage

2 sweet apples

1/2 cup sauerkraut juice

2–3 tbs fresh lemon juice

Sea salt to taste

Black pepper to taste

1/2 bunch fresh dill

2 oz walnuts

3/4 cup sour cream

1/2 tsp anise seeds

Meanwhile, wash the dill and shake dry. Remove the leaves from the stalks, and chop the leaves. Coarsely chop the walnuts.

To make the dressing, stir together the sour cream, chopped dill, walnuts, anise seeds, and wheat germ oil, and season with salt and pepper. Stir the dressing into the salad, seasoning again with salt and pepper to taste.

Tough company

If the cabbage you're using seems a little too firm or tough, heat the sauerkraut and lemon juices before pouring them over the cabbage. Let the mixture stand for about 1 hour until cool; then, mix in the grated apple and remaining ingredients.

PER PORTION:

425 calories

9 g protein

32 g fat

24 g carbohydrates

Bulgur Salad
contains lots of lactic acid
with Garlic

Peel the garlic and cut into thin slices. Pour the stock into a saucepan, add the garlic, and bring to a boil. Add the bulgur wheat, season with salt and pepper, and simmer gently for about 5 minutes over low heat. Let cool.

Meanwhile, halve the bell pepper, and remove the stem, ribs, and seeds. Rinse off the pepper segments, cut them lengthwise into strips, then cut the strips into squares. Wash and shake dry the parsley, pull the leaves from the stalks, and coarsely chop the leaves. Add the bell pepper, parsley, olive oil, borage oil, and capers to the bulgur and mix well.

Finely crumble the feta cheese over the bulgur mixture. Mix and season well with salt and pepper, adding a little more stock if the salad needs moistening. Arrange on plates and serve.

Serves 2:

4 cloves garlic

1 1/4 cups vegetable stock (plus more if necessary)

4 oz bulgur wheat

Sea salt to taste

Black pepper to taste

1 red bell pepper

2 bunches fresh Italian parsley

1 tbs olive oil

1 tsp borage oil

2 tbs capers (drained)

4 oz feta cheese

Bulgur

Bulgur is crushed dried wheat, which cooks up like rice. You will find it in most health-food stores and supermarkets. It contains large amounts of protein and B-complex vitamins.

PER PORTION:

470 calories

23 g protein

19 g fat

55 g carbohydrates

Goat Cheese
with cucumber and borage oil
Sandwich

Peel and halve the cucumber, and scoop out the seeds with a spoon. Grate half of the cucumber; cut the other half into fairly thin slices. Peel and finely chop the onion. Wash and shake dry the borage or watercress, then finely chop.

In a bowl, mix the borage oil, onion, borage leaves or watercress, grated cucumber, and goat cheese until the mixture is smooth.

Spread the cheese mixture over 2 slices of the bread, dividing evenly, and top with the sliced cucumber, pressing down slightly. Season with salt and pepper, sprinkle with the sunflower kernels, and serve open-faced, or topped with 2 additional bread slices for a brown-bag lunch.

Serves 2:
1/2 cucumber
1 small onion
A few fresh borage leaves or watercress sprigs
2 tbs borage oil
4 oz soft goat cheese
2-4 slices whole wheat bread
Sea salt to taste
Black pepper to taste
1 tbs sunflower kernels

Goat cheese

Goat cheese contains less cholesterol than other types of cheese—keeping the circulatory system healthy—and is easier to digest than cow's milk cheese. It also contains lots of vitamin A, which keeps the skin smooth and the eyes shining.

PER PORTION:

305 calories

17 g protein

19 g fat

16 g carbohydrates

Salmon and Cress
fights skin irritations
Sandwich

Serves 2: 2 whole-grain rolls • 1 bunch peppercress • 1/4 cup crème fraîche • 1 tsp borage oil • Sea salt to taste • Black pepper to taste • 1 tsp fresh lemon juice • 4 slices smoked salmon

Cut the rolls in half. Rinse the cress under cold running water, and snip off the leaves, reserving some for garnish. Mix the cress with the crème fraîche, borage oil, salt, pepper, and lemon juice, and spread on the halved rolls. Top with the smoked salmon slices, dividing evenly, and garnish with the remaining cress.

PER PORTION: 330 calories • 22 g protein • 17 g fat • 22 g carbohydrates

Dry-Cured Beef
with sauerkraut and horseradish
Sandwich

Serves 2: 2 tbs grated horseradish • 1/4 cup cottage cheese • 1 tsp pumpkin seed oil • 1 tbs chopped pumpkin seeds • 2 slices seeded bread • Black pepper to taste • 2 oz sauerkraut (drained) • 6 slices dry-cured beef (such as Swiss Bundnerfleisch)

Mix the horseradish, cottage cheese, oil, and pumpkin seeds. Spread over the bread, dividing evenly, and sprinkle with pepper. Chop the sauerkraut and divide over the cottage cheese. Fold the meat slices in half and arrange on the sauerkraut.

PER PORTION: 230 calories • 18 g protein • 9 g fat • 17 g carbohydrates

Tuna and Egg
with capers and olive oil
Sandwich

Serves 2: 1 can tuna (6 oz) • 3 tbs olive oil • 1 hard-boiled egg (peeled) • 1 tbs fresh lemon juice • 2 tbs capers • Black pepper to taste • Worcestershire sauce to taste • 2 whole-wheat rolls • 2-3 leaves radicchio

Drain the tuna. In a blender, blend the tuna, egg yolk, and lemon juice to a paste. Pour into a bowl and stir in the capers, pepper, and Worcestershire. Halve the rolls and spread with the tuna paste. Wash and dry the radicchio, cut into strips, and arrange on the rolls. Chop the egg white and sprinkle over the tops.

PER PORTION: 515 calories • 27 g protein • 33 g fat • 28 g carbohydrates

Pesto-Mozzarella
with rye bread and fresh basil
Sandwich

Serves 2: 2 slices rye bread • 2 tsp prepared pesto • 1 tbs sesame seeds • 1/2 bunch fresh basil • 6 oz fresh mozzarella cheese • 8 cherry tomatoes • Freshly ground black pepper to taste

Spread the bread with the pesto, and sprinkle with the sesame seeds. Wash and shake dry the basil, remove the leaves from the stalks, and divide the leaves among the bread slices. Drain the mozzarella, cut into slices, and place on top of the basil, dividing evenly. Wash and halve the tomatoes, remove the stalks, and arrange on top of the mozzarella, dividing evenly. Sprinkle with pepper and serve.

PER PORTION: 275 calories • 19 g protein • 16 g fat • 13 g carbohydrates

Lamb Cutlets
stimulating and full of minerals
with Vegetables

Soak the arame or dulse in 1/2 cup water for 5 minutes. Rinse and pat dry the meat. Peel and finely chop the ginger, then mix it with the dry mustard, soy sauce, lemon juice, and the 2 tablespoons water. Brush the mustard mixture over the meat. Wash and trim the remaining vegetables. Halve the leek lengthwise and slice into fine rings. Peel the carrots and cut into fine strips. Break the ends off the sugar snap peas or beans, and remove any strings.

Drain the arame or dulse well. Heat the canola oil in a nonstick skillet over medium-high heat, and brown the meat on both sides. Add the leek, carrots, peas or beans, and the arame or dulse. Season with salt and pepper, and stir-fry for about 5-7 minutes, until the meat and vegetables are cooked through. Season with soy sauce and add stir in the sesame oil. Serve with the potatoes, wild rice, or millet.

Serves 2:

2 tbs arame or dulse

1/2 cup plus 2 tablespoons water

10 oz lamb cutlets

Walnut-sized piece fresh ginger

1 tsp dry mustard

1 tbs soy sauce, plus more to taste

2 tbs fresh lemon juice

1 leek

7 oz carrots

5 oz sugar snap peas or green beans

1 tsp canola oil

Sea salt to taste

Black pepper to taste

Soy sauce to taste

1 tbs sesame oil

Cooked potatoes, wild rice, or millet, for accompaniment

power

PER PORTION: 330 calories • 50 g protein • 15 g fat • 43 g carbohydrates

Potato Pancake
with feta cheese and hot red chile
with Smoked Oysters

Wash the potatoes, and boil them in salted water to cover for about 10 minutes (they will be undercooked). Rinse under cold water, then peel. Cool the potatoes slightly, then grate coarsely.

Serves 2:

14 oz baking potatoes
Sea salt to taste
1 green onion
1 small red chile
1 clove garlic
3 sun-dried tomatoes
2 cans smoked oysters (3.7 oz each)
2 oz feta cheese
Black pepper to taste
Olive oil for frying

Meanwhile, wash and trim the green onion and chile. Cut the onion into thin rings, and finely chop the chile. Peel and finely chop the garlic, finely dice the tomatoes, and drain the oysters (chop them if desired). Crumble the feta cheese into a bowl, and mix with the grated potato, green onion, chile, garlic, tomatoes, and oysters. Season well with salt and pepper.

Heat 1-2 tbs olive oil in a nonstick skillet, and spread the potato-oyster mixture over the base of the skillet. Press down firmly with a spatula, cover with a lid, and fry over low heat for about 7 minutes, until golden brown. Carefully turn the pancake, and fry the other side until golden, adding more oil if necessary. Cut into wedges to serve.

Chiles

The spiciness of chile peppers stimulates digestion and circulation, and helps to prevent infection. Chile pods are incredibly hot, especially the white pith and the seeds inside. Avoid contact with the skin, particularly the nose and eyes. After handling chile peppers, wash your hands thoroughly to prevent burning, or wear plastic gloves.

PER PORTION:

560 calories

28 g protein

14 g fat

82 g carbohydrates

Mashed

with spiced herring, radishes, and fresh chives

Potatoes

Soak the Matjes in water for at least 1–2 hours. Wash the potatoes, and boil them in salted water to cover for about 20-30 minutes, until tender. Drain the potatoes, peel, and set aside.

Meanwhile, wash and shake dry the chives, then chop finely. Wash the radishes, setting aside 4, plus a few of the tender leaves, for garnish. Trim and dice the remaining radishes. In a saucepan, heat the potatoes with the milk and canola oil over medium heat, until just simmering. With a potato masher, mash the potatoes coarsely. Stir in the chives and diced radishes, season with salt and pepper, and heat through. Remove the fish from the soaking water, pat dry, and arrange on plates with the mashed potatoes and reserved radishes. Sprinkle the chopped radish leaves on top, and serve.

Serves 2:

4 Matjes herring fillets

14 oz baking potatoes

Sea salt to taste

1 bunch fresh chives

1 bunch radishes

1/2 cup acidopholous milk (or more if needed)

1 tbs canola oil

White pepper to taste

Matjes

Matjes are small red herring fillets, which have been spiced and brined. They are particularly delicate, and contain plenty of omega-3 fatty acids. Eating Matjes is especially good for skin radiance.

PER PORTION:

625 calories

31 g protein

44 g fat

27 g carbohydrates

Millet Spaghetti
with saffron and sesame
with Carrots

Wash the carrots and a handful of the green tops. Trim and peel the carrots, and slice them into long strips with a vegetable peeler. Peel and finely chop the onion and garlic. In a skillet, heat the sesame oil over medium-low heat. Add the sesame seeds and stir until light golden brown. Add the onion and garlic, and sauté over medium heat until the onion is translucent.

Serves 2:
9 oz fresh, green-topped carrots
1 onion
1 clove garlic
1 tbs sesame oil
2 tbs sesame seeds
Sea salt to taste
Black pepper to taste
Small pinch of ground star anise
Pinch of powdered saffron
1/2 cup orange juice
8 oz millet spaghetti

Add the carrot strips and season with salt, pepper, and star anise. Cover tightly and simmer gently over low heat for 1-2 minutes. In a small bowl, mix the saffron with the orange juice. Add the juice and green carrot tops to the pan, and stir. Simmer gently for another 2-3 minutes over low heat.

Meanwhile, cook the pasta in plenty of boiling salted water until slightly firm to the bite (*al dente*). Drain, and mix with the cooked carrot mixture. Arrange on plates and serve immediately.

PER PORTION: 560 calories • 22 g protein • 11 g fat • 93 g carbohydrates

Pasta and
with blue cheese-tomato sauce
Sea Vegetables

Soak the arame or dulse in the water for 5 minutes. Meanwhile, cut an X into the round ends of the tomatoes and plunge them into boiling water for a few moments. Remove the skins and

Serves 2:

2 tbs arame or dulse

1 cup water

1 lb ripe tomatoes

1 onion

2 tbs wheat germ oil

2 tbs tomato paste

Sea salt to taste

8 oz millet spaghetti

1-2 tbs lemon juice

5 oz blue cheese

(rind removed)

Soy sauce, black pepper, and

sweet paprika to taste

stalks, and puree in a blender. Peel and finely chop the onion. In a large rimmed skillet, heat 1 tbs of the oil over medium heat. Add the onion and sauté until translucent. Stir in the pureed tomato and tomato paste, and simmer briefly over low heat.

In a large saucepan, bring plenty of salted water to a boil. Drain the arame or dulse, and add it to the water with the spaghetti, cooking until the spaghetti is slightly firm to the bite, *al dente*. Drain, rinse under cold water, then drain again. Toss the spaghetti mixture with the lemon juice and the remaining 1 tbs oil. Crumble the cheese and melt it in the tomato sauce. Season the sauce well with soy sauce, pepper, and paprika. Add a little water to the sauce if it is too thick. Arrange the spaghetti mixture on plates, top with the sauce, and serve.

Blue cheese

Blue cheese is injected with cultures and then left to mature, until it has developed its characteristic blue-green veins. It is full of protein, easy to digest, and its enzymes have a beneficial effect on intestinal flora, and on digestion in general.

PER PORTION:

810 calories

33 g protein

43 g fat

73 g carbohydrates

power

Green Veggie

with appearance-enhancing asparagus

Ragout

Wash the cucumber, and cut in half lengthwise. Scoop out the seeds with a spoon, and cut into 1/2-inch slices. Wash and trim the asparagus, carefully peel the lower third of the stalks, and cut into 3/4-1-inch pieces. Trim and pick over the arugula, then wash, shake dry, and finely chop. Wash, shake dry, and pick over the spinach, break off any coarse stalks, and roughly chop. Peel and finely chop the onion and garlic. In a skillet, heat the oil over medium heat. Add the onion and garlic and sauté until translucent. Add the asparagus and the cucumber. Season with salt, pepper, and nutmeg, and cover tightly. Simmer gently for about 10 minutes over low heat. Add the spinach and the arugula, season with salt and pepper, and simmer for another 3 minutes. Divide the vegetables among serving plates, drizzle with the borage oil, and grate the cheese over the top.

Serves 2:

1 cucumber

9 oz asparagus

1 bunch fresh arugula

9 oz fresh spinach

1 onion

1 clove garlic

1 tbs olive oil

Sea salt to taste

Black pepper to taste

Ground nutmeg to taste

2 tsp borage oil

2 oz Parmesan cheese

Asparagus

Asparagus contains aspartic acid and potassium, which stimulate the kidneys and help the body to expel excess liquid (diuretic). It is also extremely low in calories, and is excellent for a weight-reducing diet, provided it is prepared with low-fat and -calorie ingredients. Although its benefits are not dependent on the variety, green asparagus contains more vitamins than the harder-to-find white.

PER PORTION:

215 calories

17 g protein

10 g fat

13 g carbohydrates

Boiled Potatoes with

ideal for nerves and stomach

Creamy Power Spread

Wash the potatoes and place them in a saucepan with salted water to cover. Cover the pan with a lid, bring the water to a boil, and boil for about 20 minutes, until tender. Meanwhile, halve the pepper, and remove the stem, ribs, and seeds. Rinse the pepper, then cut into small squares. Peel and finely chop the shallot and garlic. Wash and shake dry the parsley, remove the leaves from the stalks, and finely chop. Place the cream cheese in a bowl and mix with the parsley, wheat germ, yeast flakes, flaxseed oil, Tabasco, and enough water to make a smooth mixture. Mix in the chopped bell pepper, the diced shallot, and the garlic. Season well, and serve with the warm drained potatoes.

Serves 2:

1 lb small red-skinned potatoes

Sea salt to taste

1 small red bell pepper

1 shallot

1 clove garlic

1 bunch fresh Italian parsley

8 oz low-fat cream cheese

1 tbs wheat germ

1 tbs yeast flakes

1 tbs flaxseed oil

Tabasco sauce to taste

About 1/2 cup spring water

Potatoes–getting down to the roots

Potatoes contain plenty of valuable plant protein and vitamin C, and are thus an important ingredient in a powerfood plan. Raw potato juice, which is available from health-food stores, is excellent for the stomach, and is an ideal remedy for over-acidity in the system. Served with cream cheese, potatoes are similar in nutrients to a small steak, and the fiber they contain stimulates the digestion. Do not eat uncooked potatoes, as they contain indigestible starches.

PER PORTION:

335 calories

25 g protein

9 g fat

41 g carbohydrates

Turkey Breast

tender and mildly spicy

with Endive

Cut the turkey breast against the grain into 1/2-inch slices. Season with salt, pepper, and paprika. Wash and trim the endive, and cut in half lengthwise. In a saucepan, melt the butter over medium-high heat and sauté the endive until just brown at the edges. Add the turkey and brown on all sides. Add the tomatoes and season with salt and pepper. Cover tightly and simmer gently for 5 minutes over low heat. Meanwhile, peel the ginger and garlic, and slice them thinly. Add them to the skillet along with the bean sprouts and sesame oil. Drain the mozzarella, cut into slices, and place on the endive. Simmer gently over low heat until the cheese melts. Arrange on plates and serve accompanied by the baguette.

Serves 2:

7 oz boneless turkey breast

Sea salt to taste

Black pepper to taste

Sweet paprika to taste

2 heads Belgian endive

1 tsp butter

1/2 can (14.5 oz can) diced tomatoes

Walnut-sized piece fresh ginger

1 clove garlic

4 oz bean sprouts

1 tbs sesame oil

4 oz fresh mozzarella cheese

Baguette for accompaniment

Belgian endive

Endive's bitter constituents stimulate the stomach, spleen, liver, and gall bladder, making it a veritable spa food. Its components—including special carbohydrates known as "fos" (*fructooligosaccharides*)—influence intestinal health and help regenerate the membranes and flora of the intestine.

PER PORTION:

350 calories

40 g protein

17 g fat

10 g carbohydrates

Spicy Beef Stir-Fry

spicy and wonderfully stimulating

with Avocado

Combine the lemon juice, salt, pepper, a pinch of paprika, and the star anise in a shallow bowl. Cut the meat into thin strips against the grain, and place in the bowl, turning to coat the meat. Slit open the chile, remove the stem and seeds, rinse, and finely chop. Halve the bell pepper, remove the stem, ribs, and seeds, rinse, and coarsely chop. Peel and finely chop the garlic and onion.

Drain the meat. In a wok or large skillet, heat the oil over medium-high heat, add the meat, and brown on all sides. Add the chile, a pinch of paprika, the garlic and onion, and stir-fry for 5 minutes. Wash and shake dry the parsley, remove the leaves from the stalks, and chop. Halve the avocado, remove the pit, and chop. Mix the avocado, olives, and parsley, and season to taste with lemon juice, salt, and pepper. Divide the beef mixture among serving dishes, top with the avocado mixture, and serve with the desired accompaniment.

Serves 2:

3 tbs fresh lemon juice, plus more to taste

Sea salt to taste

Black pepper to taste

Hot paprika

1/2 tsp ground star anise

7 oz lean beef

1 small red or green chile

1 green bell pepper

2 cloves garlic

1 onion

1-2 tbs olive oil

1 bunch fresh Italian parsley

1 avocado

10 black olives (pitted)

Boiled millet, brown rice, or crusty bread for accompaniment

Avocado

Avocado is a tonic for the stomach, nerves, skin, and hair—provided it is ripe, and as soft as butter. Avocado contains valuable plant oils, and lots of B-complex vitamins. Mashed with a few drops of lemon juice, salt, and pepper, it makes an ideal spread, dip, or sauce.

PER PORTION:

390 calories

26 g protein

26 g fat

17 g carbohydrates

Salmon
with feta and fresh dill
on Fennel

Serves 2:
2 small salmon fillets
(about 7 oz each)
2 tbs cider vinegar
Sea salt to taste
Black pepper to taste
1 small bulb fennel
14 oz baking potatoes
1/2 bunch fresh dill
1 tbs wheat germ oil
1/2 cup plus 2 tbs water
1 tbs fennel seeds
4 oz feta cheese

Wash and pat dry the salmon fillets. Sprinkle them with the vinegar, then season with salt and pepper. Wash and trim the fennel, and cut into thin slices. Reserve a little of the green fennel tops. Wash and peel the potatoes, and cut into 1/2-inch cubes. Wash and shake dry the dill, remove the leaves from the stalks, and combine with the reserved fennel tops. In a saucepan, heat the oil over medium heat. Add the fennel and sauté for 2-3 minutes. Add the potatoes, and season with salt and pepper. Add the water and fennel seeds, and simmer for 5 minutes. Sprinkle the dill and fennel leaf mixture over the fish, and place the fish in the pan on top of the potato mixture. Crumble the feta over the top, cover tightly, and simmer everything gently for another 15 minutes, until the potatoes and fish are cooked through. Check periodically to see that there is still liquid in the pan.

Cider vinegar—modern medicine

There's a good reason why cider vinegar is currently so popular: it fights putrefactive bacteria in the intestine, kills germs, aids detoxification, and improves digestion. It is also slightly milder than wine vinegar, so it is excellent in the kitchen.

PER PORTION:

525 calories

55g protein

20 g fat

28 g carbohydrates

Sweet and Sour

with coconut and pineapple

Shrimp Fried Rice

In a saucepan, stir the rice over medium-high heat until slightly toasted. Add the water and salt, and bring to a boil. Cover tightly and simmer over low heat for 20 minutes, until the liquid is

Serves 2:
1/2 cup brown basmati rice
1 cup water
1 tsp sea salt
2 small carrots
1/2 red bell pepper
1 green onion
Walnut-sized piece fresh ginger
1 small, or 1/4 large fresh pineapple
1-2 tbs canola oil
3 tbs grated unsweetened coconut
4 oz bean sprouts
6 oz shrimp, peeled and deveined
Soy sauce to taste

absorbed. Meanwhile, wash, trim, and peel the carrots, then cut into slices. Halve the bell pepper, remove the stem, ribs, and seeds, rinse, and cut into squares. Trim the green onion and cut into thin rings.

Peel the ginger and cut into very thin strips. Peel and halve the pineapple, remove the brown "eyes" and core, and chop the flesh.

In a wok or large skillet, heat the oil over medium-high heat. Add the carrots, pepper, and green onion, and stir-fry briefly, then gradually add the coconut, ginger, and bean sprouts, stirring continuously. Add the cooked rice, pineapple, and the shrimp, and stir-fry until the shrimp just turns opaque. Season with soy sauce and serve immediately.

Sprouted soybeans

Sprouting improves the constituents of the soybean: it increases the vitamin content, breaks down protein, makes the fat more digestible, and encourages the growth of enzymes. After sprouting, the calorie content also drops.

Per Portion:

600 calories

26 g protein

24 g fat

70 g carbohydrates

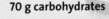

Radicchio and
with lentils and prunes
Fish Stew

Wash and pat dry the fish fillets, drizzle with cider vinegar, and season with salt. Trim the leek and slit it open lengthwise. Wash it well and cut into thin slices. Cut the prunes lengthwise into quarters. In a skillet, heat the oil over medium heat. Add the leek and sauté until glazed. Add the stock, salt, bay leaf, peppercorns, cloves, prunes, and lentils. Cover tightly and simmer over low heat for about 8 minutes; the lentils will still be slightly firm. Meanwhile, trim and wash the radicchio, and cut the leaves into strips. Add the radicchio and the fish, with the marinade, to the lentils, and simmer gently for another 3-4 minutes over low heat.

Stir in the honey and season with salt. Arrange on plates and serve with the baguette.

Serves 2:

10 oz mild white fish fillets

3 tbs cider vinegar

Sea salt to taste

1 leek

10 prunes (pitted)

1 tbs canola oil

2 1/2 cups fish or vegetable stock

1 bay leaf

3 peppercorns

2 whole cloves

2/3 cup French green lentils

1 head radicchio (about 5 oz)

1 tsp honey

Baguette for accompaniment

Radicchio

Radicchio tastes—and works—like the bitters you might find in a bar. Raddichio's constituents stimulate the digestion, and at the same time are soothing and cleanse the blood. Radicchio is related to, and is just as calming, as endive (see page 50). It's only drawback it that it loses much of its lovely red color when cooked.

PER PORTION:

525 calories

43 g protein

9 g fat

65 g carbohydrates

Chinese
with fresh fish and vegetables
Fondue

Wash and pat dry the fish, and cut it crosswise into $1\frac{1}{4}$-inch strips. Then, cut each strip into $1\frac{1}{2}$-inch pieces. Peel and finely chop the ginger. Trim, wash, and thinly slice the green onion. Squeeze the juice from the lime and reserve 1 teaspoon of the juice. Mix the remaining juice with the ginger and sliced green onion. Drizzle the ginger mixture over the fish, season with salt and pepper, and refrigerate until ready to eat. Wash and trim the sugar snap peas, and slice them on the diagonal. Wipe clean the mushrooms. Wash and halve the bell pepper, then remove the stem, ribs, and seeds. Slice the pepper on the diagonal. Put the sugar snap peas, mushrooms, and bell pepper in the refrigerator until ready to eat.

At serving time, heat the stock with the remaining 1 teaspoon lime juice and the lemon grass, until simmering. Light the heat source for the fondue pot. Pour the stock into the fondue pot, and place over the heat source. Put the fish and the vegetables in bowls around the fondue pot. Using fondue forks or small skimmers, cook the fish and vegetables in the stock and eat immediately. Accompany with rice, soy sauce, and sauces of your choice.

Serves 2:

14 oz Norwegian salmon-trout (arctic char) fillets

Walnut-sized piece fresh ginger

1 green onion

1 lime

Sea salt to taste

Black pepper to taste

7 oz sugar snap peas

7 oz small white or shiitake mushrooms

1 red bell pepper

1 1/2 quarts chicken stock

2-3 stalks lemon grass

Hot cooked rice, soy sauce, and dipping sauces of your choice as accompaniments

PER PORTION: 315 calories • 65 g protein • 10 g fat • 52 g carbohydrates

Eggplant and
with spicy tomato sauce
Shrimp Roll-Ups

Wash the eggplant, remove the stalk, and cut in on the diagonal into thin slices.

Sprinkle the slices with salt, pile the slices into two equal stacks, and weight them

Serves 2:

1 small eggplant (about 7 oz)

Sea salt to taste

8 jumbo shrimp, peeled and deveined

1 red chile

1 shallot

1 clove garlic

Juice of 1/2 lemon

2 tbs olive oil

7 oz tomatoes

1 tsp honey

1 tsp black cumin oil

1 tsp prepared pesto

Crusty bread as accompaniment

down with a cutting board. Rinse and drain the shrimp. Cut open the chile lengthwise, remove the seeds, then rinse and chop finely. Trim and finely chop the shallot. Peel and finely chop the garlic. Combine half each of the chile, shallot, and garlic with the lemon juice and 1 tbs of the oil, and drizzle over the shrimp. Cut an X into the round ends of the tomatoes and plunge them into boiling water for a few moments. Remove the skins, cut the tomatoes in half, remove the seeds, and chop coarsely. Mix the tomatoes with the remaining chile mixture, the honey, and black cumin oil, and season with salt and pepper.

Squeeze the liquid from the eggplant, wipe dry each slice with paper towels, and brush with pesto. Place the eggplant and the shrimp on a hot griddle or flat skillet, and brown on both sides; the shrimp is done when it just turns opaque. Roll the shrimp in the eggplant slices and serve with the tomato mixture and bread.

 Good options

You could also cook this dish on a grill, or under the broiler. Marinated salmon-trout (page 57) or beef (page 51) are excellent alternatives to the shrimp.

PER PORTION:

180 calories

10 g protein

12 g fat

8 g carbohydrates

power

Steamed Fresh
in a creamy broth
Mussels

Wash the mussels, scrubbing them thoroughly, and carefully remove any attached hairy filaments (beards). Discard any shells that are open.

Peel the onion and slice into rings. Trim and wash the celery, and cut into slices.

In a large skillet, heat the oil over medium heat. Add the onion, and sauté until translucent. Add the celery, and sauté briefly. Peel and crush the garlic, and add it to the skillet. Add the mussels and vegetable stock, and bring to a boil. Cover tightly and cook for about 8 minutes. Remove the mussels when all the shells have opened, and keep warm.

Serves 2:
- 2 lb mussels
- 1 onion
- 1-2 stalks celery
- 1 tbs canola oil
- 1 clove garlic
- 2 cups vegetable stock
- 1/3 cup sour cream
- Sea salt to taste
- Black pepper to taste
- 1/2 bunch fresh Italian parsley
- Crusty bread for accompaniment

Pass the mussel cooking liquid through a fine strainer into a clean saucepan, and cook over high heat until reduced to about a third of the original volume. Stir in the sour cream and just heat through. Season with salt and pepper.

Wash and shake dry the parsley, remove the leaves from the stalks, and chop the leaves. Sprinkle the parsley over the sauce. Return the mussels to the broth, and accompany with the bread for dipping.

power

PER PORTION: 225 calories • 15 g protein • 15 g fat • 8 g carbohydrates

The New Balanced Diet

The Natural

between acid and alkaline

Balance

ACID, ALKALINE, AND pH

Do you sometimes feel "sour" – even "acidic"? Or do you simply feel worn out? The reason for this could be a less-than-ideal balance between acid and alkaline elements in your body. Chemically speaking, an acid always contains the free, positively charged water particles: H+. An alkali consists mainly of negatively charged particles with a single water atom and a single oxygen atom: OH-. The level of acid and alkaline is measured in pH. If this figure is 7, the positively and negatively charged particles are balanced, or neutral. The alkaline level rises from 7 to 14, and the acid level falls from 7 to 0.

ACID AND ALKALINE
IN THE BODY

The pH values in our bodies differ from organ to organ. This is because certain reactions occur only at a specific pH level. In the stomach, where hydrochloric acid is produced, the pH value is very acid. The gall bladder and pancreas also produce acids. Alkaline digestive juices are produced solely in the saliva and in the duodenum. The pH value can vary tremendously throughout our connective tissue, but it must remain more or less stable at 7.4 in the blood–slightly alkaline; otherwise our metabolism would break down. Our body has a buffer system to ensure it stays at the desired alkaline level, no matter how well or how poorly we eat. By constantly discharging acids through the lungs, kidneys, digestive organs, and skin, our bodies maintain the proper acid-alkaline balance.

IF THE BALANCE IS WRONG

In a healthy body, acid and alkaline are well balanced. However, stress, unhealthy eating, and too little rest and relaxation can have such an effect on this balance that we start to feel unwell. Our modern lifestyles tend to increase the production of acid in the body: fast food, high-protein foods (such as meat, cheese, and fish), sweets, alcohol, coffee, and tobacco, all produce large amounts of acid. To make things worse, we rush around all day, neglect to breathe properly or get enough exercise, and do not eat enough alkaline forming foods to help our bodies achieve the proper balance.

DO I HAVE TOO MUCH ACID?

Because our bodies have such good buffers, we never really become overly "acidic." However, latent over-acidity can become a chronic condition and, in time, put our bodies under great stress. Excessive acid can accumulate in the tissues, where it is

difficult to find, but it still makes its presence known. The circulation diminishes, and tissues become slack. The body itself soon shows the symptoms of over-acidity; frequent heartburn, gastritis, exhaustion, backache, a "spongy" feel to the skin, and brittle hair and fingernails are all typical signs.

HOW TO FIND OUT FOR YOURSELF

The pH content of the urine changes throughout the course of a day. It is affected by the amount of sleep we get, as well as by what we eat and drink. Ideally, the pH level of our urine should be somewhere between 5 and 8. Urine is generally more acidic in the morning and evening, and more alkaline at midday and in the afternoon. To get an idea of your internal chemistry, you can measure the acidity in your urine before and after every meal and before you go to bed. You can find the test strips at your local drugstore. On contact with urine, the strips will change color at a pH level between 5 and 8. If the figures are outside this range, follow our "Power Week" eating plan (see page 128), and measure again at the end of the seven-day period. The best proof, however, is how much better you'll feel after changing to an alkaline-forming diet. The principles laid out in the plan can be incorporated into your eating plan for life.

Living the

What works – and how

Alkaline Way

Food's Potential

Depending on its composition, all food that we eat produces a certain amount of acidic or alkaline substances in our bodies. For example, protein is highly acid forming, carbohydrates are alkaline forming, and fats are neutral. Minerals too, can be positively or negatively charged, and affect the acid or alkaline balance in the body. The processes of the digestive system also contribute to the end result of acid or alkaline balance. Determining the acid- or alkaline-forming potential of a particular food is not foolproof. However, the tables on pages 6 and 7 can be used as a rough guide.

Acid-Forming Substances

Many foods and drinks that we consume to rev up our systems actually cause our bodies' pH level to drop; for example, alcohol, coffee, soda, and improperly brewed tea can all cause excess acid in the system. Chocolate, candy, cakes, cookies, refined sugar, and white flour are also acid forming. Consuming meats, fish, shellfish, cheese, and eggs also lead to a buildup of acid in the system. Conversely, a vegetarian diet is highly alkaline promoting.

The Neutrals

Our bodies need neutral substances because they contain vital nutrients. Neutral foods include cultured milk products and milk with added calcium. Butter, clarified butter, and cold-pressed oils with added vitamin E and beta-carotene are also neutral substances. Amaranth, spelt, millet, quinoa, and buckwheat are all full of protein and vitamin B, and are an ideal substitute for the more common types of grains, as well as acid-forming rice.

Beneficial Alkaline forming Foods

With just a few exceptions, fruit, potatoes, and vegetables are highly alkaline. Even if some foods taste acidic, such as citrus fruits, they can have an alkaline effect on the body. This also applies to vegetables that contain lactic acid, such as sauerkraut.

There are vast differences between the different types of legumes; although flageolet beans are alkaline forming, most dried legumes are acid forming. Opinions differ with regard to nuts and seeds, but almonds, pumpkin seeds, and sunflower seeds are alkaline forming–and the fresher they are, the better.

Note: Sprouts are always alkaline, and therefore very healthy. Furthermore, fresh sprouts are full of vitamins, minerals, and bioactive substances.

WHAT SHOULD I DRINK?

It's important to make sure you drink enough fluids, as they are beneficial for the kidneys and help the body to flush away acids. Ideally, you should drink at least 2 quarts of liquid per day. Noncarbonated mineral water is a good choice, as are mild herbal teas. Special alkaline-forming teas are sold in health food stores. Black tea, provided it is left to brew for at least four minutes, is a sound choice. Natural fruit and vegetable juices are alkaline forming, but almost count as a snack, and are best diluted with water. Among milk products, choose buttermilk or acidopholous milk.

WHAT ABOUT SNACKS?

Constantly adding undigested food to the semi-digested food already in our stomach can cause heartburn and over-acidity. It is therefore better to stick to three meals a day, with perhaps a little fruit in between if you are really hungry. Low-fat granola and salads are ideal, alkaline-forming cold meals. Sandwich ingredients, however, are usually highly acid forming. Instead, opt for some Spelt and Potato Bread with a vegetarian spread (see pages 136–137).

Balanced
foods to remember for a balanced diet
Foods

Several factors determine whether a food is acid- or alkaline-forming, such as its mineral content, its effect on the body's metabolic system, and its effects on the digestive organs. The following table is intended as a guideline.

NOTE: To achieve and maintain the ideal balance, the food you eat should be 80 percent alkaline forming and 20 percent acid forming. Eat neutral foods in moderation, and choose those that are low-fat.

REMEMBER: Foods that taste acidic don't necessarily have an acidic effect on the body. Citrus fruit, kiwi, and pineapple are, like most fruits, highly alkaline forming. Vegetables that contain lactic acid, such as sauerkraut, capers, pickled gherkins, and olives, are alkaline forming even though they taste acidic.

ALKALINE FORMING

potatoes

most fresh vegetables

fresh fruit

dried fruit

honey

fruit syrups

maple syrup

cane sugar

sprouts & seeds

herbs and spices (cinnamon, bay leaves, vanilla, marjoram, dill, mustard, cumin)

sauerkraut

capers

olives

yeast

soy sauce

herbal teas

noncarbonated water

NEUTRAL TO SLIGHTLY ALKALINE FORMING

milk

acidopholous milk

buttermilk

yogurt

cream

soy milk

tofu

millet

buckwheat

amaranth

quinoa

potato flour

arrowroot

egg yolks

butter

cold-pressed oils

vinegar

sunflower seeds

pumpkin seeds

NEUTRAL TO SLIGHTLY ACID FORMING

spelt

whole-grain crackers

sourdough bread

green beans

brown rice

sesame seeds

cashew nuts

pistachios

almonds

hazelnuts

fresh cheeses

cottage cheese

sour milk products

beer

dry wine

ACID FORMING

meats and sausages

fish

shellfish

egg whites

aged cheese

white flour

light-colored breads

pasta

rice

corn

refined sugar

chocolate

candy

peanuts

walnuts

Brussels sprouts

artichokes

carbonated drinks

alcoholic beverages

coffee

black tea (brewed for less than one minute)

Power

Eating and drinking the alkaline way

Week

CHANGE THE HABITS OF A LIFETIME

Do life's stresses make you feel like escaping to a desert island? Instead, try this basic eating plan for a week, and see if you still feel the same way at the end of it. Excess acid will be eliminated from your body and you will soon start to feel fit and relaxed. It could be the beginning of a new, healthier way of life. In time, you can gradually re-introduce dairy products and normal grains to your diet. If you decide to follow this plan for the long term, be sure to take calcium supplements.

THE ONE-WEEK BALANCING PLAN

The weekend before you start, bake some Spelt and Potato Bread*, make some Potato and Almond Spread and Mixed Fruit Puree, and prepare some Vegetable Stock. Buy the ingredients for Ginger and Nettle Tisane, and a mountain of fruit. Drink at least 2 quarts of spring water, and as much vegetable stock as you like every day. You can also prepare for the week by eating only fruit and vegetables on the Sunday before you begin the plan to detoxify your system. In the Power Week's plan, there are three main meals per day and two "extras," which you can eat either at mealtimes or as snacks in between; make sure you leave at least two hours between meals. Incidentally, you may experience headaches and weariness, and generally feel down when you first begin the plan. Hold out—in no time you'll start to feel better. And last, but not least: if you find you are still hungry after a meal, eat twice the amount next time.

✹ Hint: Freeze the bread in portions so that it remains fresh all week.

THE WEEK'S MEALS

Monday

* 1 slice of Spelt and Potato Bread with Potato and Almond Spread; Mixed Fruit Puree * Curried Potato Pancake * Buckwheat-Stuffed Tomatoes with 2 slices of Spelt and Potato Bread * Berry Milkshake

Tuesday

* Muesli with Spelt and Millet * Winter Bean Stew * Arugula and Wild Rice Salad with 1 slice of Spelt and Potato Bread * Pumpkin Salsa Verde with raw or steamed vegetables

Wednesday

* 2 slices of Spelt and Potato Bread with Potato and Almond Spread and butter; Mixed Fruit Puree or honey * Potato and Tomato Cocktail; Fresh Plum Dumplings * Roasted Fennel with Exotic Mushrooms; boiled new potatoes and Quinoa and Butter Lettuce Salad * Pear Milkshake with Cinnamon

Thursday

* Mixed Fruit Granola * Creamy Asparagus Dip with boiled new potatoes * Provençal Vegetable Salad with 2 slices of Spelt and Potato Bread * Cream of Basil Soup

Friday

* Muesli with Fresh Berries * 1 slice of Spelt and Potato Bread with Potato and Almond Spread or Honeyed Fresh Fruit * Potato-Apple Gratin; Dandelion Salad with Kidney Beans and 1 slice of Spelt and Potato Bread * Chocolate Pudding

Saturday

* 1–2 slices of Spelt and Potato Bread with Honeyed Fresh Fruit; Berry Milkshake * Vegetable Tempura with tomato sauce; Marinated Peppers * Green Pasta Salad with Potato and Tomato Cocktail * Red Currant Sorbet Float

Sunday

* 1–2 slices of Spelt and Potato Bread with Honeyed Fresh Fruit; Potato and Almond Spread * Beet Ragout; Tomato and Asparagus Salad * Cream of Pumpkin Soup

Honeyed

also delicious with

Fresh

citrus fruits

Fruit

Serves 4: 1/3 cup honey • 1 kiwi • 1 nectarine • 1 tbs fresh lemon juice • 4 oz fresh strawberries or raspberries • 2 tbs fresh blueberries

Spread 2–3 tablespoons of the honey over the bottom of a flat dish. Peel the kiwi and cut into 1/4-inch slices. Slice the nectarine and sprinkle with lemon juice. Pick over the berries, wash if necessary, and pat dry. Spread the fruit over the honey and cover with the remaining honey. The fruit will keep for 1 week if stored in an airtight container in the refrigerator.

TOTAL: 123 calories • 1 g protein • 1 g fat • 32 g carbohydrates

Ginger and Nettle
diuretic, invigorating, and alkaline forming
Tisane with Licorice

Makes about 1 quart: 1 finger-sized piece fresh ginger • 1 piece licorice root • 3 tbs nettle tea • Freshly ground nutmeg to taste • 1 quart boiling water • 1 orange

Finely chop the ginger and licorice and place in a teapot with the tea and some freshly ground nutmeg. Pour over the boiling water and let steep for 10 minutes. Wash the orange, cut it into slices, and place in heat-resistant glasses. Strain the tisane over the orange slices. Drink the tisane hot or cold.

TOTAL: 18 calories • 0 g protein • 1 g fat • 4 g carbohydrates

Berry
flavored with vanilla bean
Milkshake

Serves 2: 4 oz berries (fresh or frozen) • 1 cup cold acidopholous milk • 1 vanilla bean • 1-2 tbs fruit syrup or honey

Sort and wash the berries, then drain. Place in a blender with the milk. Slit the vanilla bean open. Using a sharp knife, scrape the seeds from the pod and add to the berry mixture. Add the syrup or honey and blend all the ingredients well. Pour into tall glasses and serve with straws.

PER DRINK: 130 calories • 5 g protein • 3 g fat • 23 g carbohydrates

Pear Milkshake

mild tasting and rich in calcium

with Cinnamon

Serves 2: 1 pear • 1 cup cold whole milk • 1/2 tsp ground cinnamon • 1-2 tsp floral honey

Wash and peel the pear. Cut it into quarters, and remove the core and stem. With a blender, process the pear with the milk, cinnamon, and honey until smooth. Pour into tall glasses and serve with straws.

PER DRINK: 132 calories • 5 g protein • 5 g fat • 21 g carbohydrates

Potato and Tomato

with acid-binding potato juice

Cocktail

Serves 2: 1 lb potatoes, or 1/2 cup potato juice • 1 tbs cider vinegar • 2 fresh basil leaves • 2 tbs capers with liquid • 1 cup tomato juice • Pinch of herbed salt mix • Black pepper

Wash, peel, and puree the potatoes. Sprinkle the vinegar over the potatoes and let stand for 10 minutes before passing through a fine sieve; Or, combine the potato juice and vinegar. Wash the basil leaves and pat dry. Finely chop the capers and basil leaves. Combine with the potato mixture, tomato juice, salt, and pepper. Serve immediately in cocktail glasses.

PER DRINK: 72 calories • 3 g protein • 1 g fat • 16 g carbohydrates

Spelt and

with alkaline-forming ingredients

Potato Bread

Wash the potatoes, and steam them for 20-30 minutes, until tender. Peel the potatoes while still hot and push through a potato ricer into a large bowl. Combine the spelt flours and the yeast, and add them gradually to the mashed potatoes, mixing well.

Makes 2 loaves:
1 lb baking potatoes
1 lb spelt flour
1 lb whole-grain spelt flour
2 packets rapid-rise yeast
Lukewarm water
2 tbs salt
1 tsp ground cumin
8 oz sunflower kernels

If the dough seems too stiff, thin it with a little water; the dough should have a soft, malleable consistency. Shape it into a ball in the bowl. Cover the bowl and let the dough rise at room temperature for 1 hour. Add the salt, cumin, and half of the sunflower kernels. Knead the dough gently to mix in the ingredients.

Grease the insides of 2 loaf pans and sprinkle with half of the remaining sunflower kernels. Divide the dough in half, place it in the pans, and sprinkle with the remaining sunflower kernels. Place the loaves in the bottom of a cold oven, turn the heat to 400°F, and bake for about 1 hour, until the loaves sound hollow when thumped. Let the loaves cool in the pans, then remove.

PER PORTION:

202 calories

8 g protein

5 g fat

31 g carbohydrates

Potato and
with fresh basil and garlic
Almond Spread

Wash the potatoes, and steam them for 20-30 minutes, until tender.

Meanwhile, steep the almonds in boiling water for a few minutes, then

Makes one 10-oz jar:
8 oz baking potatoes
2 oz whole almonds
1 bunch fresh basil
1 clove garlic
4-5 tbs olive oil
1 tsp salt
Black pepper to taste

rinse in cold water and remove the skins. Wash the basil, shake dry, and tear off the leaves. Peel and crush the garlic. Puree the almonds, olive oil, basil, garlic, salt, and pepper with a blender or food processor until smooth.

Peel the hot potatoes and blend to a paste with the basil-almond mixture. Add salt and pepper to taste. The spread will keep for 3-4 days in a tightly capped jar in the refrigerator.

Potatoes

In folk medicine, potatoes are regarded as a universal panacea. Although highly alkaline, they are full of protein. Grain protein is an ideal accompaniment, so bread topped with this savory potato spread can definitely hold its own against a steak sandwich. To retain their nutrients, potatoes are best steamed in their skins, rather than peeled and boiled.

power

TOTAL:

830 calories

16 g protein

68 g fat

42 g carbohydrates

Mixed Fruit

contains no acid-forming sugar

Puree

Makes one 10-oz jar: 4 oz pitted prunes • 4 oz raisins • 4 oz dried figs • 1/2 cup orange juice

• Ground cinnamon to taste

Wash the prunes, raisins, and figs in hot water, drain on paper towels, and chop. Place in a bowl, pour over the orange juice, and let stand for 1 hour. Puree the mixture in a blender and season with cinnamon. Store in the refrigerator in an airtight container. Keeps for up to 2 weeks.

TOTAL: 800 calories • 9 g protein • 3 g fat • 193 g carbohydrates

Uncooked Mixed-

alkaline forming when sweetened with honey

Fruit Jam

Makes one 10-oz jar: 8 oz red currants • 4 oz strawberries • 1/4-1/2 cup honey

Pick over and wash the red currants and strawberries, and drain them thoroughly. Strip the currants from the stalks and press them through a coarse sieve. Cut any large strawberries into smaller pieces. Beat the red currant puree, strawberries, and honey to taste in an electric mixer for 10 minutes, until the mixture begins to thicken. Store in a tightly capped sterilized jar in a cool, dark place. Keeps for 4-6 weeks.

TOTAL: 576 calories • 3 g protein • 1 g fat • 138 g carbohydrates

Muesli with Spelt
with tangy citrus
and Millet

Place the grains and poppy seeds in a saucepan with the water and simmer gently for 1 minute. Cool, then chill until ready to use.

Serves 2:
3 tbs coarsely ground spelt
3 tbs coarsely ground millet
2 tbs poppy seeds
1 cup water
1 small banana
1 cup milk
1 pink grapefruit
1 orange

Peel the banana, blend with the milk, and combine with the grains. Divide the grain and milk mixture among two bowls.

Peel the grapefruit and orange with a very sharp knife, removing all of the bitter white pith. Cut down the sides of each membrane to release the fruit segments. Arrange the fruit pieces on the muesli and serve immediately.

Grains

As well as good quantities of fiber, vitamins, and bioactive substances, grains also contain *phytin,* an acid that prevents minerals and–probably–vitamins from being absorbed in the digestive tract. Phytin loses its efficacy when cooked, baked, or sprouted, which is why freshly ground or flaked cereals should be both boiled and soaked before eating. Ready-flaked cereals have already been cooked.

PER PORTION:

272 calories

10 g protein

7 g fat

43 g carbohydrates

power

Mixed Fruit
with popped amaranth
Granola

Serves 2:
1 large apple
2 dried figs
6 dried apricots
1 cup water
1 cinnamon stick
1-2 tbs honey
8 tbs popped amaranth

Wash and peel the apple. Cut it in half and remove the core, then chop into small pieces. Wash the figs and apricots, drain, and chop into small pieces. Place the figs and apricots in a saucepan with the apple, water, and cinnamon and bring to a boil. Simmer gently, covered, for about 5 minutes. Stir in the honey. Let the apple puree cool and remove the cinnamon stick. Divide the apple puree among two dishes and serve immediately topped with the popped amaranth.

Amaranth

Amaranth, a seed from the Andes, is less acid forming than many other grains and is high in protein. Since it contains no gluten, it is not suitable for baking with yeast, unless combined with wheat flours. Amaranth is available popped from specialty and health food stores. It is also available in whole-grain form, which can be ground either in the store or, if you prefer, by yourself at home.

PER PORTION:

282 calories

5 g protein

3 g fat

65 g carbohydrates

power

Sprouted Muesli
invigorating and low in calories
with Fresh Berries

Place the seeds in a preserving jar, cover with warm water, and soak for 24 hours. Drain the seeds, rinse, and return to the jar. Fill the jar with water and let stand for a few minutes. Cover the jar with a double layer of cheesecloth and secure with a rubber band. Place the jar upside down on a rack in the sink to allow the water to drain away. Set the jar aside and let stand for about 5 days, until the seeds form small shoots and delicate sprouts appear.

Serves 2:

4 oz millet seeds (easy sprouting)

1 cup fresh seasonal berries

2/3 cup plain yogurt

1-2 tbs maple syrup

Sprinkle the sprouts with water daily. When relatively large, wash the sprouted seeds thoroughly and drain.

Pick over and wash the berries, then drain. Combine the berries with the tiny millet shoots. Combine the yogurt and maple syrup, mixing until smooth and creamy, then pour over the berry-sprout mixture.

Sprouted seeds

Sprouting reduces the amount of fat and *phytin* and increases the vitamin and mineral content of seeds. Sprouted seeds are less acid forming than unsprouted seeds and are perfectly digestible when raw. Wash the sprouts thoroughly in a sieve before eating. You can also stir-fry them or blanch them in boiling water.

PER PORTION:

193 calories

6 g protein

4 g fat

34 g carbohydrates

Arugula and Wild Rice Salad

a lovely dinner, snack, or brown-bag lunch

Peel and finely chop the ginger and onion. Rinse the lime under hot water, pat dry, and carefully remove the zest in strips, avoiding the white pith; set aside. Squeeze the juice from the lime. Mix the lime juice with a drop of honey, some pepper, and the green peppercorns. Marinate the onion and ginger in the lime mixture overnight.

Place the wild rice in a saucepan with the water, salt, cumin, and reserved lime zest, and bring to a boil. Simmer over low heat for 45 minutes. Let cool, then remove the zest.

Wash the arugula and cut into bite-sized pieces; wash and slice the radishes. Place the wild rice, arugula, and radishes in a bowl. Stir together the ginger-onion mixture and the oil, season to taste with salt and pepper, and pour over the salad, tossing well. Arrange the salad on plates and serve.

Serves 2:

1 piece fresh ginger (thumb-sized)
1 red onion
1 lime
Honey to taste
Pepper to taste
1 tsp green peppercorns
1/2 cup wild rice
1 cup water
Salt to taste
1/2 tsp ground cumin
1 bunch arugula
1 bunch radishes
3-4 tbs canola oil

PER PORTION: 350 calories • 9 g protein • 17 g fat • 44 g carbohydrates

Quinoa and

with mushrooms and horseradish

Butter Lettuce Salad

Serves 2:
3/4 cup quinoa
2 tbs olive oil
1/2 cup vegetable stock
1 small bay leaf
1/2 tsp fresh thyme leaves
1/2 head butter lettuce
8 oz mushrooms
1 small onion
1/2 clove garlic
1/2 lemon
5 tbs heavy cream
1 tbs sour cream
1 tsp creamy-style horseradish
Salt to taste
Black pepper to taste

In a skillet, sauté the quinoa in 1 tbs of the oil, until toasted. Add the vegetable stock, bay leaf, and half of the thyme. Simmer gently for 15 minutes, remove from the heat, and let cool.

Wash and drain the lettuce. Wash or wipe clean the mushrooms and cut into slices.

Peel and finely chop the onion and garlic. Finely grate the lemon zest and squeeze out the juice.

To make the dressing, whip the cream until stiff. Add the sour cream and lemon juice. Season with the lemon zest, the remaining half of the thyme, the horseradish, salt, and pepper.

Heat the remaining 1 tbs oil in a skillet and sauté the onion, mushrooms, and garlic, until softened. Season with salt and pepper.

Carefully mix half of the dressing with the cooled quinoa. Divide the lettuce leaves among two plates and drizzle with the remaining dressing. Divide the quinoa among the lettuce beds. Arrange the mushroom mixture on top and serve.

PER PORTION: 528 calories • 19 g protein • 20 g fat • 66 g carbohydrates

Dandelion Salad
soothes body and mind
with Kidney Beans

Soak the beans in the water overnight. The next day, drain and rinse the beans and replace the water with a fresh supply. Add the rosemary and bay leaf and bring to a boil. Simmer the beans for 1 1/2 hours, until tender. Add the salt, and let cool.

Grate a couple pinches of orange zest. With a thin, sharp knife, peel the whole orange, removing all the bitter white pith. Cut down the sides of each membrane to release the fruit segments (make sure you collect the juice). Squeeze the juice from the 1/2 orange and set aside with the collected juice.

Wash, peel, and dice the carrots. Heat the oil in a saucepan and sauté the carrots until softened. Season to taste with salt and pepper, add a small amount of orange juice, and simmer gently for about 8 minutes, until tender.

Serves 2:
1/2 cup dried red kidney beans
2 cups cold water
1 sprig fresh rosemary
1 small bay leaf
Salt to taste
1 1/2 oranges
4 oz carrots
1 tbs vegetable oil
Pepper to taste
1 bunch fresh chives
4 oz dandelion greens
2 tbs Dijon-style mustard
1 tbs brown mustard
1/4 cup heavy cream

Wash the chives and dandelion greens. Chop the chives, and combine with the dandelion greens, orange segments, diced carrots, and drained beans. Season well. Mix the mustards and cream with the remaining orange juice and orange zest. Season with salt and pepper. Serve the dressing with the salad.

PER PORTION: 384 calories • 16 g protein • 15 g fat • 46 g carbohydrates

Tomato and
with alkaline forming mustard powder
Asparagus Salad

Wash the asparagus and snow peas. Peel the lower third of the asparagus stalks and cut the asparagus into 2-inch pieces; set the tips aside separately.

Add some salt and the lemon juice to the water and bring to a boil. Boil the lower pieces of asparagus for 5 minutes, then add the asparagus tips and the snow peas, and cook until tender-crisp, about 3-5 minutes. Drain, reserving the cooking liquid, and place in ice water to cool.

Meanwhile, wash the tomatoes and cut into eighths. Wash and shake dry the tarragon. Remove and discard the coarse stalks, and chop the rest. Pass the egg yolk through a fine sieve and combine with the mustard and enough of the asparagus cooking liquid to make a dressing. Whisk in 1 tbs of the oil, and half of the chopped tarragon. Season with salt and pepper.

Toss the tomatoes, snow peas, and drained asparagus with the dressing and arrange on plates. Break the bread into small pieces. Heat the remaining 2 tbs oil in a skillet over medium heat and sauté the bread until brown on all sides. Sprinkle over the salad. Garnish with the remaining tarragon and serve immediately.

Serves 2:

9 oz white or green asparagus

3 oz snow peas

Salt to taste

1 tbs fresh lemon juice

1/2 cup water

2 tomatoes

1/2 bunch tarragon

1 hard-cooked egg yolk

1 tsp dry mustard

3 tbs extra virgin olive oil

Pepper to taste

3-4 thin slices stale bread

PER PORTION: 172 calories • 5 g protein • 11 g fat • 14 g carbohydrates

Roasted Fennel with

with herbes de Provence

Exotic Mushrooms

Preheat the oven to 400°F. Wash the fennel and cut in half. Remove the green tops from the fennel and set aside. Place two pieces of aluminum foil, shiny side up, on the work surface, rub

Serves 2:

2 bulbs fennel (about 10 oz each)

2 tbs extra virgin olive oil, plus more for greasing foil

1/2 tsp herbes de Provence

4 oz assorted mushrooms, such as brown (cremini), oyster, and/or chanterelle

2 tbs fresh lemon juice

1 clove garlic

1/4 cup dry white wine

Salt to taste

Black pepper to taste

with oil, and sprinkle with the herbs. Place two fennel halves, cut side down, on each piece of foil. Firmly seal the foil over the top of the fennel. Roast in the center of the oven for 35 minutes, until tender.

Wash and finely slice the mushrooms and sprinkle with 1 tsp of the lemon juice. Peel and thinly slice the garlic. Heat 1 tbs of the oil in a skillet over medium-high heat and sauté the mushrooms until tender. Add the wine, heat through, and transfer to a bowl.

Wipe out the skillet, add the remaining 1 tbs oil, and gently sauté the garlic. Season well with the remaining lemon juice, salt, and pepper, and combine with the mushrooms. Unwrap the fennel, cut into thin slices, and arrange on plates with the mushrooms and fennel greens. Refrigerate, covered, for 2 to 3 hours. Serve at room temperature.

Fennel

Fennel is alkaline forming and aids the body in breaking down acids. It contains 2-3 percent essential oils, which stimulate the circulation in the digestive tract and respiratory system, and strengthen the stomach, kidneys, and liver. Fennel is most effective eaten raw.

PER PORTION:

145 calories

5 g protein

8 g fat

8 g carbohydrates

Marinated
with chopped hazelnuts
Peppers

Preheat the grill to high (you can also use a broiler). Wash the peppers and pat dry. Grill the peppers (or cook on a baking sheet under the broiler), turning occasionally, until the skins turn black and start to blister on all sides. Remove the peppers from the grill and sprinkle with salt. Cover with a damp tea towel and let stand until cool enough to handle. Holding the peppers over a bowl, remove the charred skins, collecting any juice that exudes. Cut the peppers lengthwise into 8-10 pieces, removing the stalks, ribs, and seeds. Peel and roughly chop the garlic. Squeeze the lime and mix the juice with the pepper juices and the olive oil. Season well with the garlic, salt, pepper, and paprika. Add the pepper strips and marinate for at least 30 minutes.

Wash the parsley and shake dry. Remove the parsley leaves and roughly chop. Divide the marinated pepper strips among serving plates and sprinkle with the parsley and hazelnuts.

Serves 2:
1 red bell pepper
1 yellow bell pepper
1/2 green bell pepper
Salt to taste
1 clove garlic
1/2 lime
2 tbs extra virgin olive oil
White pepper to taste
Hot paprika to taste
1/2 bunch fresh Italian parsley
1 oz chopped hazelnuts

Peppers

Bell peppers are not just highly alkaline; the chemical *capsaicin*, prevalent in the pepper family, stimulates the circulation and digestion, beta carotene strengthens the body's resistance, and bioflavinoids stabilize the blood vessels.

PER PORTION:

185 calories

4 g protein

15 g fat

10 g carbohydrates

Provençal
lavender adds special flair
Vegetable Salad

Wash the beans and wash and peel the potatoes. Trim the beans, removing any strings. In a saucepan, bring the water and 1/2 tsp salt to a boil. Add the beans and potatoes and cook for 30 minutes, until tender. Trim the zucchini and cut into small pieces. Halve the pepper, remove the stem, ribs, and seeds, and cut the flesh into small pieces. Peel the onion and garlic and finely chop.

Mix together the olive oil, vinegar, pepper, mustard, and lavender. Add some of the vegetable cooking water to the dressing and season to taste.

Peel and slice the potatoes. In a bowl, pour the dressing over the potatoes and beans. Stir in the zucchini, onion, and garlic, and chill. Wash the basil and shake it dry. Pull the leaves from the stalks and tear them into rough pieces.

Cut the radicchio into bite-sized pieces.

Wash and drain well. Add the basil, olives, and radicchio to the salad. Toss and season well.

Serves 2:
4 oz green beans
8 oz boiling potatoes
1/2 cup water
Salt to taste
1 zucchini
1 red bell pepper
1 red onion
1 clove garlic
3 tbs extra virgin olive oil
2 tbs white wine vinegar
Pepper to taste
1 tbs mustard
1 tbs chopped fresh lavender leaves and flowers
1 bunch fresh basil
1 small head radicchio
10 black olives (pitted)

PER PORTION: 335 calories • 10 g protein • 15 g fat • 45 g carbohydrates

Green
revitalizing and highly alkaline
Pasta Salad

Serves 2:
4 oz millet pasta
Salt to taste
4 oz baby spinach
5 oz zucchini
1/2 bunch fresh basil
6 green olives (pitted)
1 clove garlic
1/4 cup vegetable stock
2 tsp fresh lemon juice
Pepper to taste
1-2 tbs freshly grated
Parmesan cheese

Cook the pasta in a large amount of boiling salted water until slightly firm to the bite (al dente). Drain and rinse under cold water. Wash the spinach and the zucchini. Pick over the spinach, remove any hard stalks, and drain. Slice the zucchini thinly.

Wash the basil, shake dry, and tear off the leaves. Peel the garlic. Puree the basil leaves in a blender with the olives, stock, and lemon juice. Season the dressing with salt and pepper.

In a bowl, combine the pasta, spinach, and zucchini. Add the dressing and toss carefully. Arrange the pasta salad on 2 plates, sprinkle with the cheese, and serve.

Spinach

Spinach is one of the most alkaline-rich vegetables. It contains large amounts of iron and folic acid, and its high copper content encourages blood formation. The hormone *secretin* stimulates the pancreas. Spinach also contains oxalic acid, which binds calcium (this is what causes the rough feeling on the teeth). For maximum benefit, drink milk or calcium-enriched fruit juice when you eat spinach.

PER PORTION:

280 calories

15 g protein

8 g fat

39 g carbohydrates

Quinoa Salad with

a slightly alkaline evening meal

Creamy Vinaigrette

In a saucepan, briefly sauté the quinoa in 1 tsp of the olive oil. Add the lemon juice, water, and 1 tsp salt. Bring to a boil, cover tightly, and simmer gently for 15 minutes. Cool.

Peel and finely grate the beets. Grate the cheese coarsely. Wash the chives, shake dry, and cut into small pieces. Set aside 1/2 tsp for the dressing. Peel and finely chop the garlic. Wash and finely grate the cucumber.

In a bowl, lightly mix the quinoa, beets, cheese, chives, garlic, and cucumber. In a small bowl, combine the stock, mustard, remaining 1/2 tsp chives, pepper, vinegar, remaining 3 tsp oil, and the cream until smooth. Pour the dressing over the salad just before serving, and toss well.

Serves 2:

2/3 cup quinoa
4 tsp extra virgin olive oil
Juice of 1/2 lemon
2 cups water
Salt to taste
4 oz fresh beets, cooked
3 oz pecorino Romano cheese
1 bunch fresh chives
1 small clove garlic
1 cucumber
1/4 cup vegetable stock
1/2 tsp Dijon-style mustard
Pepper to taste
1 tbs mild vinegar
1 tbs heavy cream

Quinoa

Quinoa is a cereal-like cultivated plant from South America. Its seeds are small and round, and are slightly alkaline forming. Like amaranth, quinoa contains more protein than other grains. It is also high in iron, zinc, potassium, magnesium, and vitamin C.

PER PORTION:

409 calories

18 g protein

16 g fat

48 g carbohydrates

Buckwheat-Stuffed
full of protein and minerals
Tomatoes

Wash the tomatoes, thinly slice off the tops (to use as lids), and scoop out the insides with a spoon; reserve the insides of the tomatoes for another use. Put the tomatoes upside down in a sieve to drain. Season the tomato cavities well with salt and pepper.

Lightly toast the buckwheat groats in a nonstick skillet. Wash and thinly slice the green onions. Peel and finely chop the garlic. Chop the sauerkraut into small pieces. Wash the dill and pull the tips from the coarse stalks.

In a bowl, combine the buckwheat, green onions, garlic, sauerkraut, and dill. Add the salt, pepper, lemon juice, and oil and mix carefully. Season the filling well and divide among the tomatoes. Place the "lids" on the tomatoes, arrange on plates, and serve.

Serves 2:
6 large tomatoes (about 2 lb)
Salt to taste
Pepper to taste
1/2 cup buckwheat groats
2-3 green onions
1 clove garlic
8 oz sauerkraut (drained)
1 bunch fresh dill
3-4 tbs fresh lemon juice
2-3 tbs canola oil

Variations
Use small bell peppers instead of tomatoes. Use amaranth or quinoa for the filling instead of buckwheat (boil the grains first in 1 cup vegetable stock and cool). For a Mediterranean flair, use basil or herbes de Provence instead of dill.

PER PORTION:
441 calories
13 g protein
15 g fat
66 g carbohydrates

Spicy
with zesty horseradish
Radish Dip

Serves 2: 1 bunch radishes • 1/2 cup buttermilk • 1/4 cup heavy cream • 1 tsp creamy-style horseradish • Salt to taste • Black pepper to taste

Wash the radishes and puree them in a blender, setting some of the juice aside. Mix the pureed radishes with the buttermilk. Whip the cream until stiff and combine with the radish puree. Season the dip with the horseradish, salt, and pepper. If the mixture is too thick, adjust the consistency with some of the radish juice (drink the rest) and keep the dip cool.

PER PORTION: 90 calories • 1 g protein • 8 g fat • 3 g carbohydrates

Pumpkin
with alkaline-forming olives and herbs
Salsa Verde

Serves 2: 1 bunch fresh Italian parsley • 1 bunch fresh basil • 2 oz pumpkin seeds • 2 oz green olives (pitted) • 1/2 cup vegetable stock • 2 tbs olive oil • Salt to taste • Black pepper to taste • 1 clove garlic

Wash the herbs, shake them dry, and pull off the leaves. With a blender, puree the basil and parsley leaves with the pumpkin seeds and olives, and gradually add the stock. Mix in the oil and season with salt and pepper. Peel and finely chop the garlic and stir into the salsa.

PER PORTION: 259 calories • 10 g protein • 22 g fat • 9 g carbohydrates

Creamy

with mascarpone cheese and fresh basil

Asparagus Dip

Wash and trim the asparagus, and peel the lower third of the stalks. Wash and shake dry the basil and pull the leaves off the stems.

Place the asparagus, basil, and mascarpone in a food processor or blender and puree until the mixture is smooth and creamy.

Combine the puree with salt, pepper, lemon juice, olive oil, and a small amount of the vegetable stock, to achieve a dip consistency.

Serves 2:

4 oz asparagus

1/2 bunch fresh basil

2 oz mascarpone cheese

Salt to taste

Pepper to taste

1 tbs fresh lemon juice

1 tsp olive oil

Vegetable stock

Dips

These dips are high in protein, and go well with raw or steamed vegetables, pasta, and potatoes for a highly satisfying meal. They can easily be prepared in advance and are ideal for a brown-bag lunch.

Mascarpone has a relatively high fat content, but it is less acid forming than other types of cream cheese or cottage cheese. Its high amount of valuable lactic acid makes it slightly alkaline forming. You can increase the alkaline effect by adding vegetables to the dip–such as the asparagus used in this recipe. Asparagus is also slightly diuretic, and stimulates the liver and kidneys.

PER PORTION:

145 calories

3 g protein

13 g fat

5 g carbohydrates

Gnocchi
a tasty Italian-style treat
with Tomatoes

Wash the potatoes and steam them for 20-30 minutes, until very tender. Peel the potatoes while hot and push them through a potato ricer. Let stand for a few minutes to drive off the steam. Mix in 1 tsp salt, the flour, and as much potato flour as is needed until the dough is no longer sticky. On a floured work surface, shape the dough into finger-thick rolls and cut into 1-inch pieces. With a fork, slightly flatten each piece.

In a large saucepan, bring a generous amount of salted water to a boil. Reduce the heat and simmer portions of gnocchi in the water for 4 minutes. Rinse the cooked gnocchi in cold water and drain. Keep warm on a baking sheet in a very cool oven (175°F).

Peel and quarter the shallots. Sauté them in a skillet with 1 tbs of the butter, cover with a lid, and simmer with the orange juice for 8 minutes, until glazed.

Serves 2:
Generous 1 lb baking potatoes
Salt to taste
3 tbs flour
2-3 tbs potato flour
3 shallots
2 tbs butter
1/4 cup orange juice
12 oz ripe tomatoes
1/2 bunch fresh sorrel
1 tbs tomato puree
Honey to taste
Mild paprika to taste
Pepper to taste

Meanwhile, cut an X into the round ends of the tomatoes and plunge them into boiling water for a few moments. Remove the skins, cut the tomatoes in half, and remove the seeds. Cut the tomato flesh into strips. Wash and pick over the sorrel and cut into strips. Add the tomato puree, honey, paprika, and the remaining 1 tbs butter to the shallots. Add the tomato strips and sorrel and heat through. Season with salt and pepper and serve with the hot gnocchi.

PER PORTION: 322 calories • 9 g protein • 6 g fat • 58 g carbohydrates

Tomato and Red

with thyme and basil

Pepper Sauce

Wash the tomatoes, remove the stalks, and cut into eighths. Cut the red pepper in half and remove the stem, ribs, and seeds. Wash it and cut it lengthwise into 4-6 pieces. Peel, halve, and chop the onion.

In a skillet, heat the olive oil over medium heat and sauté the onion gently until translucent. Stir in the tomato and red pepper. Add the tomato puree, honey, thyme, salt, and pepper, and simmer for 30 minutes.

Remove the thyme and puree the sauce in a blender. Simmer the sauce, uncovered, until thick. Season to taste with salt and pepper. Add the basil just before serving.

Serves 2:
Generous 1 lb ripe tomatoes
1 small red bell pepper
1 onion
2 tbs olive oil
1 tbs tomato puree
1 tsp honey
1/2 sprig fresh thyme
Salt to taste
Black pepper to taste
2 tbs chopped fresh basil

Tomatoes

Tomatoes, like peppers, are highly alkaline forming. They also contain high amounts of potassium and magnesium, which support the kidneys and have a diuretic effect. The antioxidant *lycopene* strengthens the immune system. A thickened tomato sauce is an ideal alkaline-forming spread, and is delicious on toasted bread.

PER PORTION:

140 calories

4 g protein

7 g fat

16 g carbohydrates

Cream Sauce
elegant and very aromatic
with Morels

Serves 2: 3/4 oz dried morels • 1 cup water • 1 shallot • 1 tsp butter • 1 cup vegetable stock • 1/2 tsp cornstarch • 1/4 cup heavy cream • Salt to taste • White pepper to taste

Soak the morels in the water for 8 hours, then wipe clean. Strain the soaking water through a paper coffee filter and reserve. Peel and chop the shallot and sauté it gently in the butter until translucent. Add the morels and simmer briefly. Add the soaking liquid and the stock, and bring to a simmer. Dissolve the cornstarch in the cream. Pour into the mushroom mixture, heat carefully, stirring, until thickened. Season with salt and pepper.

PER PORTION: 116 calories • 1 g protein • 10 g fat • 5 g carbohydrates

Carrot and
a creamy, alkaline-forming topping
Almond Sauce

Serves 2: 7 oz carrots • 1 onion • 1 tbs butter • 1 oz ground almonds • 2 tbs tomato puree • 1/2 cup vegetable stock • Salt to taste • Pepper to taste • Freshly grated nutmeg to taste • 1/4 cup heavy cream • Yeast flakes (optional)

Wash, peel, and grate the carrots. Peel and dice the onion. Sauté the carrots and onion in the butter, until the onion is translucent. Add the almonds, tomato puree, and stock. Season with salt, pepper, and nutmeg and simmer for 5 minutes. Puree in a blender. Stir in the cream and sprinkle with the yeast flakes (if using).

PER PORTION: 212 calories • 4 g protein • 17 g fat • 11 g carbohydrates

Winter Bean

with plenty of vegetable protein

Stew

Chop the tomatoes into small pieces and soak overnight in the water with the beans, bay leaf, and peppercorns.

Serves 2:
3 dried tomatoes
2 1/4 cups water
4 oz dried flageolet beans
1 bay leaf
A few black peppercorns
1 leek
9 oz potatoes
1 clove garlic
Salt to taste
1 oz pumpkin seeds
1-2 tbs pumpkin seed oil
1-2 tbs cider vinegar

In a saucepan, cook the tomatoes and the beans in the soaking water for 30 minutes.

Meanwhile, wash the leek and potatoes. Trim the leek and cut into slices. Peel the potatoes and cut into small dice. Peel and finely chop the garlic.

Add everything to the pan with the beans. Season the stew with salt and cook for about 20 more minutes, until the potatoes are soft.

Toast the pumpkin seeds in a dry nonstick skillet, until golden brown. Add them to the stew with the pumpkin seed oil and cider vinegar. Season with salt.

Seasonal stews

A delicious summer alternative is to make this stew with fresh beans and tomatoes instead of dried ones, and use 1 bell pepper and 2 green onions instead of the leek. In spring, substitute 2-3 baby carrots, and 2 bunches of fresh sorrel for the leek. Or, use 9 oz chopped spinach and 1 chopped onion.

Per Portion:

398 calories

20 g protein

16 g fat

46 g carbohydrates

power

Cream of
with potatoes and garlic
Basil Soup

Serves 2: 9 oz potatoes • 1 onion • 1 clove garlic • 1 tbs butter • 2 cups buttermilk • Salt to taste • White pepper to taste • 1-2 tsp arrowroot • 1 bunch fresh basil • 2 tbs sour cream

Wash the potatoes. Peel and finely chop the potatoes, onion, and garlic. In a skillet, sauté the potatoes and onion in the butter until they start to turn brown. Add the buttermilk, season to taste, and simmer for 20 minutes. Mix the arrowroot with 2 tbs water. Add to the potato mixture, bring to a boil, and stir until thickened. Wash the basil, tear off the leaves, and add them to the soup. Carefully puree the mixture and serve garnished with the sour cream.

PER PORTION: 166 calories • 4 g protein • 4 g fat • 28 g carbohydrates

Cream of
satisfying and highly alkaline-forming
Pumpkin Soup

Serves 2: 1 1/2 lb pumpkin flesh • 1 onion • 1 tbs olive oil • Salt to taste • Pepper to taste • 1 cup carrot juice • 2 tbs crème fraîche • Ground ginger to taste • Fresh lemon juice to taste • 1 oz dried currants • 1/2 oz roughly chopped pumpkin seeds

Roughly chop the pumpkin flesh. Peel and finely chop the onion. Add both to a saucepan with the oil, season with salt and pepper, and sauté over medium heat until tender. Puree with the carrot juice and crème fraîche. Season with the ginger and lemon juice. Add the currants and pumpkin seeds, heat through, and serve.

PER PORTION: 247 calories • 6 g protein • 13 g fat • 28 g carbohydrates

Vegetable
a tasty base for sauces, stocks, and stews
Stock

Peel and chop the onions. Wipe clean the mushrooms and cut into slices. Sauté the onions and mushrooms in a large saucepan without oil until they turn dark.

Wash, trim, and chop the remaining vegetables. Add them to the pan with the water, salt, bay leaves, cloves, peppercorns, and herbs and bring to a boil.

Simmer the vegetables over low heat for 1 hour and let cool. Ideally, let the stock stand overnight in the refrigerator. Pass the liquid through a sieve and season well. The stock will keep for up to 1 week in a sealed container in the refrigerator.

Makes about 1 quart:

2 large onions

4 oz mushrooms

1 carrot

1 stalk celery

1 leek

2-3 ripe tomatoes

5 cups water

1 tsp salt, plus more to taste

2 bay leaves

2 whole cloves

1 tsp black peppercorns

1 sprig fresh rosemary

2 sprigs fresh thyme

Mushrooms

This stock tastes especially good if you chop the mushrooms, sprinkle them with salt, and let them stand for 24 hours. This allows them to ferment, turning brown and highly aromatic. Dried mushrooms have a similar effect. You can sip the stock either hot or cold. For an extremely delicious creamy-style vegetable soup, add carrots, pumpkin, or potatoes, cook, and puree.

Per Portion:

27 calories

1 g protein

1 g fat

1 g carbohydrates

Vegetable Tempura

gently cooked veggies in a crispy coating

In a small bowl, combine the flours. In another bowl, mix the egg yolk, half egg white, about 1/4 cup of the flour mixture (more if needed), the ice water, salt, and oil to a smooth paste. Refrigerate until ready to use.

Wash and dry the tomatoes. Wipe the mushrooms clean. Wash and trim the leek and cut into finger-width slices. Wash again if necessary. Place the vegetables in the refrigerator for 1 hour.

Coat the vegetables in the remaining flour and then coat them with the batter. Heat about 1 inch of oil in a small saucepan. When hot, add the vegetables and fry until golden brown; drain on paper towels.

Sprinkle lime juice over the vegetables and serve with soy sauce for dipping.

Serves 2:
1/4 cup amaranth flour
1/4 cup spelt flour
1 egg yolk
1/2 egg white
1/2 cup ice water
Salt to taste
1 tsp olive oil
4 oz cherry tomatoes
5 oz small white mushrooms
1 large leek
Vegetable oil
Soy sauce

Deep-fried vegetables

It is important that all the ingredients are cold before frying. Also suitable for tempura: broccoli florets, snow peas or sugar-snap peas, strips of bell pepper, slices of zucchini or eggplant, and asparagus.

PER PORTION:

350 calories

11 g protein

21 g fat

30 g carbohydrates

Curried Potato
with exotic carrot dip
Pancake

Wash, trim, and thinly slice the green onions. Peel and finely chop the garlic, setting one-third aside for the dip. Peel and finely grate the ginger.

Serves 2:

- 2-3 green onions
- 2 cloves garlic
- 1 nut-sized piece fresh ginger
- 1 1/4 lb potatoes
- Salt to taste
- White pepper to taste
- 1-2 tsp curry powder
- 2 tbs chopped cashew nuts
- 2 tbs clarified butter or olive oil
- 7 oz carrots
- Grated orange zest to taste
- 1/2 cup plain yogurt
- 1 tbs pumpkin seed oil

Wash, peel, and coarsely grate the potatoes. Stir in the green onions, garlic, and ginger. Season well with salt, pepper, and curry powder.

Toast the cashew nuts in a large nonstick skillet with 1 tbs of the clarified butter or oil. Place the potato mixture on top, cover with a lid, and fry gently for 10 minutes. Flip over, adding the remaining 1 tbs clarified butter or oil, and fry until brown.

Meanwhile, peel and puree the carrots. Combine with the remaining garlic, the grated orange zest, yogurt, pumpkin seed oil, and salt and pepper to taste. Cut the potato pancake into serving wedges and serve with the carrot dip.

PER PORTION: 488 calories • 11 g protein • 25 g fat • 54 g carbohydrates

Beet

with buckwheat blinis

Ragout

Mix the flour with the cold water. Stirring constantly, add the warm water, yeast, honey, and 1/2 tsp salt, and let stand for 1 hour.

Wash and peel the beets and cut into 2 inch strips. Peel the onion, cut in half crosswise, and slice thinly. Wash, peel, and halve the apple. Remove the core and cut into segments. Sprinkle with lemon juice. In a saucepan, heat 1 tbs of the oil and add the onion, beets, allspice, and stock and simmer for 10 minutes. Add the apple segments and simmer, uncovered, for 2 minutes. Season the mixture with salt and pepper.

In a skillet, heat 1 tbs of the oil over medium heat. Ladle in three 1/4-cup portions of the blini mixture and fry for 3-4 minutes, until golden brown. Turn the blinis and fry until the other side is golden brown. Remove from the pan and keep warm. Repeat with the remaining blini mixture and oil.

Toast the buckwheat groats in a dry skillet until golden. Place 3 blinis on each plate. Top with some of the beet ragout and a spoonful of sour cream. Garnish with the dill and the buckwheat, and serve immediately.

Serves 2:
3/4 cup buckwheat flour
1/2 cup cold water
1/2 cup warm water (110°F)
1 package active dry yeast
1/2 tsp honey
Salt to taste
14 oz beets
1 medium onion
1 tart apple
2-3 tbs lemon juice
3-4 tbs sunflower oil
Pinch of allspice
1/2 cup vegetable stock
Pepper to taste
3-4 tbs buckwheat groats
2 tbs sour cream
2 tbs chopped fresh dill

PER PORTION: 644 calories • 13 g protein • 30 g fat • 80 g carbohydrates

Stir-Fried
quick and nourishing
Amaranth

In a saucepan, bring the amaranth, lemon grass, and stock to a boil. Reduce the heat and simmer the amaranth for 15 minutes. Wash and trim the green onions and cut into thin slices. Wash and trim the carrots, then peel them and cut into slices. Wipe the mushrooms clean and, depending on size, cut them into four or eight pieces.

Serves 2:

1/2 cup amaranth
1 tsp dried lemon grass
1 cup vegetable stock
2 green onions
10 oz baby carrots
7 oz mushrooms
2 tbs corn oil
2 oz skinned almonds
4 oz bean sprouts
1 tbs sesame oil
Soy sauce to taste

Heat the corn oil in a wok over medium heat and stir-fry the almonds until they start to smell aromatic. Add the carrots and stir-fry briefly.

Add the mushrooms, green onions, and bean sprouts and stir-fry for 5 minutes. Add the cooked amaranth and the sesame oil, stir-fry for a moment, and add the soy sauce. Remove the lemon grass and serve immediately.

Gentle cooking with a wok

A wok is ideal for cooking small portions. Because stir-fried ingredients are cut into small pieces, and the food is cooked quickly, the nutrients are retained. This recipe can also be made with cooked millet, quinoa, or whole-wheat pasta (non-egg) instead of amaranth. Other possible vegetables include Chinese cabbage, broccoli florets, kohlrabi, spinach, beets, bell peppers, and other bean sprouts. Do not cook more than 11/4 lb at a time.

PER PORTION:

613 calories

21 g protein

41 g fat

43 g carbohydrates

power

Potato-Apple
with arugula and herbed cheese
Gratin

Serves 2:
1 lb potatoes
1/4 cup heavy cream
2 tbs herbed cheese,
such as Boursin
1 cup vegetable stock
2 tsp cornstarch
2 tbs water
Salt to taste
Pepper to taste
4 oz arugula
Butter for coating the dish
2 small cooking apples
2 oz sunflower kernels

Wash the potatoes and steam them until tender, about 20-30 minutes. In a saucepan, bring the cream, cheese, and vegetable stock to a boil. Mix the cornstarch with the water, add to the cream mixture, and stir until thick. Season well with salt and pepper and remove from the heat. Wash the arugula and shake it dry. Cut it into pieces and add to the sauce.

Preheat the oven to 400°F. Butter a small baking dish (about 1 quart capacity). Peel and slice the potatoes. Peel and halve the apples and remove the cores. Slice them into segments.

Arrange alternate layers of potato and apple in the baking dish and pour the herbed cheese mixture over the top. Sprinkle with the sunflower kernels. Bake the gratin in the middle of the oven for 30 minutes, until golden brown.

Herbs

Herbs are always alkaline—and that's not all: they are high in vitamins and minerals. Consumed in large quantities, herbs are highly therapeutic and can be used for medicinal purposes. Arugula contains large quantities of mustard oils, which aid the digestion and fight infections.

Per Portion:

407 calories

11 g protein

19 g fat

51 g carbohydrates

Baked Zucchini on

an appetizing alkaline aid

Tomato Amaranth

Place the amaranth in a saucepan with the tomato juice, a little salt and pepper, and the thyme and bring to a boil. Simmer gently over low heat for 15 minutes. Meanwhile, wash and trim the zucchini. Using a sharp knife, cut the zucchini lengthwise into fan shapes, leaving the stem intact, and gently spread the segments out.

Preheat the oven to 400°F. Grease a small baking dish (1 quart capacity) with a small amount of the oil. Mix the cooked amaranth with the remaining olive oil, pour into the gratin dish, and spread evenly with a spoon. Lay the zucchini fans on top.

Serves 2:
3/4 cup amaranth
1 1/4 cups tomato juice
Salt to taste
White pepper to taste
1/2 tsp dried thyme
1 lb baby zucchini
1-2 tbs olive oil
3 tbs ground hazelnuts
3 tbs freshly grated Parmesan cheese

Mix the hazelnuts with the Parmesan and sprinkle over the zucchini. Place the dish in the center of the oven and bake for 20 minutes, until golden brown.

PER PORTION: 584 calories • 22 g protein • 31 g fat • 58 g carbohydrates

Fresh Plum
with plum compote and hazelnuts
Dumplings

Wash the potatoes and steam them until tender, about 20-30 minutes. Peel the potatoes while still hot and push them through a potato ricer. Let stand for a few minutes to drive off the steam. Carefully mix the riced potatoes with a pinch of salt, the flour, and as much potato flour as necessary so that the mixture holds together, but is still very soft. Wash the plums. Select the 12 best and dry them. Carefully remove the stones, then push the plums together so that they appear to be intact. Divide the dough into 12 equal pieces, press a plum into the center of each piece, and gently roll into a ball. Halve the remaining plums and remove the stones. Very gently simmer the plums with 1/2 tsp of the cinnamon and the water until tender. Stir 2 tbs of the maple syrup into the compote and chill.

Serves 2:
1 lb baking potatoes
Salt to taste
3 tbs flour
2-3 tbs potato flour
14 oz small fresh plums
1 tsp ground cinnamon
2 tbs water
4 tbs maple syrup
2 tbs butter
2 tbs finely chopped hazelnuts

In another saucepan, bring a large amount of salted water to a boil. Drop the dumplings in the water and simmer, uncovered, for 10 minutes, until they rise to the top. Remove with a slotted spoon and drain.

In a skillet, heat the butter over medium heat and sauté the nuts until golden. Add the remaining 1/2 tsp cinnamon and toss the plum dumplings in this mixture. Drizzle them with the remaining 2 tbs syrup and serve with the compote.

PER PORTION: 538 calories • 8 g protein • 14 g fat • 94 g carbohydrates

Red Currant
light and refreshing
Sorbet Float

Wash and sort the red currants, remove them from the stalks, and drain.

Puree the berries and press through a sieve into a freezerproof bowl. Stir in

Serves 2:

9 oz fresh red currants

Scant 1/2 cup maple syrup

Pinch of ground cinnamon

Sparkling water

the maple syrup. Place the mixture in the freezer,

stirring every 30 minutes, until frozen.

Transfer the sorbet to the refrigerator about 30

minutes before serving. Stir the sorbet well, divide

among two glasses, and top with sparkling water.

✳ Fruity desserts

These dishes are alkaline forming, provided they do
not contain large amounts of dairy products, eggs,
white flour, gelatin, or sugar. Use agar-agar instead of
gelatin, cornstarch or arrowroot instead of flour,
cocoa powder instead of chocolate, and honey, maple
syrup, or dried fruit puree instead of refined sugar.

PER PORTION:

216 calories

1 g protein

1 g fat

51 g carbohydrates

Chocolate

sweetened with dried dates

Pudding

Serves 2: 8 dried pitted dates • 2 1/2 cups whole milk • 5 tbs unsweetened cocoa powder

• 2 tbs cornstarch • 2 tbs water

Wash the dates and puree with a blender. Place in a saucepan, and gradually add the

milk and cocoa powder. Bring to a boil, stirring constantly. Mix the cornstarch with

the water, stir into the cocoa mixture, and simmer gently for 1 minute over low heat.

Divide among 2 dessert bowls and chill until ready to serve.

PER PORTION: 314 calories • 13 g protein • 13 g fat • 51 g carbohydrates

Tropical

with lime juice and pineapple

Jelly

Serves 2: 1 small fresh pineapple • 3 oranges • 1 lime • Scant 1 tsp agar-agar • 2-3 tbs honey

Peel the pineapple and cut into slices. Remove the woody core and cut the slices into pieces.

Peel and divide 2 of the oranges into segments. Squeeze the juice from the remaining orange

and the lime. Add enough water to the juice to make 1 cup of liquid. Remove 2-3 tbs juice and

mix with the agar-agar. Bring the remaining juice mixture to a boil, stir in the agar-agar, and

boil for 1-2 minutes. Stir in the honey and fruit, pour into a mold, and chill for at least 4 hours.

PER PORTION: 162 calories • 1 g protein • 1 g fat • 38 g carbohydrates

Semifrozen
Fruit Pudding
with berried-banana puree

Combine the yogurt, vanilla, honey, and lemon zest and stir until smooth and creamy. Add the agar-agar and let stand for 15 minutes. Then, simmer the mixture gently in a small saucepan for 2-3 minutes and let cool. Stir in the egg yolk when the mixture starts to set at the edges. In a bowl, whip the cream until stiff peaks form, and fold into the pudding mixture.

Line a small mold or dish with aluminum foil (shiny side up). Grease the foil. Pour the mixture into the prepared mold and place in the freezer for at least 6 hours or up to overnight.

To serve, carefully remove the pudding from the mold, discard the foil, and let the dessert stand for 30 minutes.

Meanwhile, make the sauce: Squeeze the juice from the lemon. Peel and slice the banana and puree with the lemon juice and honey. Add the banana puree to the berries in a bowl. Serve the pudding with the berried-banana puree.

Serves 2:
1/2 cup plain yogurt
1/2 tsp vanilla extract
2 tbs clover honey
1 tsp grated lemon zest
1 tsp agar-agar
1 egg yolk
1/2 cup heavy cream
Vegetable oil for greasing the dish
For the sauce:
1 lemon
1 banana
2-3 tbs honey
1/2 pint fresh raspberries

PER PORTION: 493 calories • 7 g protein • 23 g fat • 67 g carbohydrates

Cleansing Food

Detoxify the

with artichokes, asparagus, and other cleansing foods

Natural Way

HEALTH ALL YEAR ROUND

Treating your body to an "inner spring cleaning" contributes to vitality and well-being. Delicious, detoxifying foods stimulate the metabolism, purify the blood, rid the body of excess fluid, and put the liver, gallbladder, and kidneys into tiptop working order. The traditional time for a "detox" is in the spring–the Christian practice of fasting for Lent is a typical example. In the weeks leading up to Easter, there is an abundance of foods ideal for the purpose of detoxifying, such as the first tiny artichokes and baby asparagus. However, many detoxifying foods are available all year, so you can really perform a spring cleaning in any season.

A SLUGGISH SYSTEM

Nature normally takes care of the "ins" and "outs" of the food we eat. If the "outs" part of the process is no longer functioning as well as it might, unwanted by-products and waste substances can accumulate in the body. These impurities are deposited in the blood vessels, joints, tissues, organs, and muscles, and can show in one's appearance.

In the long run, serious illnesses can result. The first indications that impurities are building up in the body are constant fatigue, lack of concentration, listlessness, chronic headache, and susceptibility to infections. Skin breakouts, frequent digestive upsets, and muscle and joint pain can also signal the need for a detox. These are warning signals given by your body—take them seriously. To combat these ailments, treat your body to a general overhaul. Carefully planned menus, conscious enjoyment of the foods themselves, sufficient exercise in the open air, adequate periods of relaxation, and a little skin and body pampering will do you good. You will emerge feeling as if you are new born.

Organs responsible for Detoxification

LIVER: The liver can be described as the body's own chemical factory—a great variety of chemical transformation processes happen here. The liver's key role is enabling the body to use the food eaten by breaking down certain substances and forming others. As bodies age, they absorb more and more harmful substances, such as alcohol, caffeine, cigarette smoke, car exhaust fumes, and other toxins. The task of putting things right falls on the liver, and if it is not in good shape, we will feel the ill effects. The liver also manufactures bile, which is particularly important for the digestion of fats.

KIDNEYS: Consider the kidneys the blood's filter. The blood flows through the kidneys many times a day to sift out any nutritionally useful substances, which are returned to the circulation, and any harmful substances that are present in excess. The latter are excreted in urine made by the kidneys. Overtaxing the body with impurities, such as medications and alcohol, or frequent urinary infections, can, in the long run, damage the kidneys and/or cause them to cease functioning.

INTESTINES: A healthy intestinal flora acts on the food in the gut, taking out any nutritionally useful substances that have not yet been digested, and leaving the useless ones to be excreted. The greatest enemies of intestinal flora are antibiotics and food with too little roughage. Both hinder the smooth functioning of the digestive processes, damage the intestinal flora, and enable metabolic breakdown products to accumulate.

LUNGS: The role of the lungs in detoxifying the body mainly involves expelling carbon dioxide, filtering out toxic substances from the air we breathe, and removing toxins present in the blood. Heavy smokers face an increased risk of damaging the lungs and affecting their detoxifying abilities.

SKIN: Healthy skin protects the body against unwanted invaders. Sweating also rids the body of harmful substances through the skin's pores.

Fitness

Detoxify yourself for a healthy feeling

Inside and Out

DAILY SELF-HELP GEMS

❋ Drink plenty of fluids. This is important to flush out the kidneys and carry away metabolic breakdown products.

❋ Keep active. Good exercise includes breathing in plenty of oxygen–the more you do this, the better your metabolism will be.

❋ Take the time to eat properly, and be sure to chew slowly. The digestion of carbohydrates begins in the mouth.

❋ Eat a low-fat diet. Fat is the last nutrient to be digested from the food, and it is a slow process. The liver will be taken up with its share of the task for a long time, leaving little time for its detoxification role.

❋ Avoid alcohol, tobacco, and medications as much as possible. Metabolizing these substances makes great demands on your body's detoxification organs.

❋ Treat commercially prepared meals as a last resort. They often contain many additives, such as flavorings and flavor enhancers, spelling hard work for the liver. They may also contain hidden fats, which will jeopardize your eating plan.

CHOOSE YOUR FOODS WISELY

❋ Eat plenty of carbohydrates, especially fiber-rich foods. The roughage present in these items promotes the activity of the intestines, making it more difficult for unwanted substances to accumulate.

❋ Select foods that provide a good amount of vitamins and minerals. These enable all the processes of the body to take place efficiently. Sufficient vitamins and minerals ensure thorough removal of waste products–the key to a detoxification plan. Some vitamins are essential components of digestive juices.

❋ Eat raw fruit and vegetables as often as you can. Cooking destroys important nutrients in these foods. Raw foods also contain quantities of certain digestive enzymes, which are beneficial to the body.

❋ Consume many base-forming foods, which will protect the body from excess acid. Raw fruit, vegetables, and salad greens are good examples. A diet too rich in acid-forming substances, such as meats, sweets, alcohol, coffee, and tea, imposes a great deal of work on the liver and kidneys.

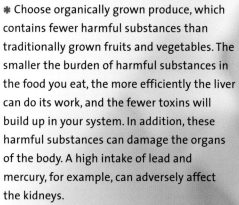

✳ Choose organically grown produce, which contains fewer harmful substances than traditionally grown fruits and vegetables. The smaller the burden of harmful substances in the food you eat, the more efficiently the liver can do its work, and the fewer toxins will build up in your system. In addition, these harmful substances can damage the organs of the body. A high intake of lead and mercury, for example, can adversely affect the kidneys.

✳ Choose fresh vegetables and fruits whenever possible. If not possible, choose frozen. Vegetables for freezing are freshly picked, so they offer the best chance of still containing their valuable nutrients.

✳ For those who wish to use them, there are several preparations to assist in simple, speedy detoxification and ridding the body of excess fluid; health food stores and pharmacies stock these. For example, artichokes and asparagus can be found as juices, or in tablet form. Other juices available are from bean, nettle, watercress, pumpkin, dandelion, parsley, black radish, and other plants with health-giving properties. Delicious, healthy cocktails can be mixed using some of these, together with fresh fruit and vegetable juices. Of course, this should be in addition to eating fresh foods.

Cleansing

Foods to remember in a detox plan

Foods

FRUIT AND VEGETABLES

ARTICHOKES: Contain *cynarin*, which stimulates the liver and gallbladder, promotes the flow of blood through them, cleanses them, and also promotes the digestion of fats. Artichokes help rid the body of excess fluid (diuretic) and lower the cholesterol level

ASPARAGUS: Contains aspartic acid, which is a strong diuretic; stimulates the kidneys; and has a positive effect on the body's metabolism. Also contains potassium, which helps rid the body of excess fluid

BELGIAN ENDIVE: Contains the bitter constituent *intybin*, which contributes to the proper function of the liver, gall-bladder, stomach, and intestines; stimulates digestion and metabolism; cleanses the system; helps rid the body of excess fluid; promotes blood formation

FENNEL: Contains volatile oils that stimulate liver and kidney activity; promotes digestion

KOHLRABI: Stimulates the flow of bile, and is beneficial to the kidneys; promotes blood formation

LEEKS: Promote digestion; cleanse the intestine; contain mustard oils, which stimulate the liver, gallbladder, and kidneys; help rid the body of excess fluid

PINEAPPLE: Contains the enzyme *bromelin*, which promotes metabolism and helps rid the body of excess fluid

POTATOES: Help rid the body of excess fluid

RADISHES: Contain volatile oils, which stimulate digestion and the formation of bile; unblock biliary flow; help rid the body of excess fluid

HERBS AND SPICES

BURNET: Helps rid the body of excess fluid (diuretic)

DILL: Stimulates urine flow

GARDEN CRESS: Purifies the blood; helps rid the body of excess fluid; stimulates metabolism

GINGER: Stimulates circulation; promotes appetite and digestion

HORSERADISH: Helps rid the body of excess fluid; stimulates stomach, gallbladder, kidneys, and intestines

JUNIPER: Purifies the blood; helps rid the body of excess fluid

LOVAGE: Stimulates the flow of bile and secretion of stomach digestive juices; promotes kidney activity

NASTURTIUM: Stimulates the formation of red blood cells; purifies the blood; encourages the transport of oxygen around the body

NETTLE: Purifies the blood; increases urine flow. Contains an excess of bases, so it's good for de-acidification

PURSLANE: Purifies the blood and helps in blood formation; helps rid the body of excess fluid

ARUGULA: Regenerates the mucous lining of the gut; helps rid the body of excess fluid

TARRAGON: Helps rid the body of excess fluid; stimulates metabolism; cleanses the kidneys and gallbladder

TURMERIC: Fortifies the liver and gallbladder; purifies the blood; increases production of bile

SUBSTANCE	EFFECT	IMPORTANT SOURCES
Bitter constituents	strengthen the glands that produce digestive juices, stimulate the gallbladder; promote the digestion of fats	broccoli, artichokes
Calcium	combats the heavy metals lead and cadmium, preventing their storage in the body	milk, nuts, broccoli, green cabbage
Chloride	regulates the acid-base balance; detoxifies	almost all foods
Fiber	stimulates the activity of the intestines, shortening the time that the food remains in the gut; absorbs metabolic and other waste products in the stomach and intestines, so that they can be eliminated	grains, leafy green vegetables, peas, carrots, potatoes, apples, pears, berries
Glutathione	speeds up detoxification processes in the body	leafy green vegetables, radishes, root vegetables
Hot constituents	stimulate digestion	spices such as ginger, chiles, pepper, paprika
Iron	promotes blood formation; important for transport of oxygen	peas, beans, spinach, nuts, cabbage, grapes, red meat
Mustard oils	have a purifying and antiseptic effect; increase activity of stomach and intestines; strengthen liver, gallbladder, kidneys, and bladder	cabbage, radishes, root vegetables, onions, leeks
Potassium	rids the body of excess fluid and stimulates kidney activity; strengthens blood vessels and kidneys	potatoes, cabbage, brown rice, fruit, grains
Secondary plant substances	protect against free radicals, which are involved in the buildup of impurities in the body; help the cleansing process; can be diuretic	fruit and vegetables
Selenium	binds heavy metals and enables their elimination from the body; stimulates the liver; important for deactivating free radicals	almost all types of fruit and vegetables, red cabbage, grains, nuts, meat
Volatile oils	stimulate the metabolism, helping to remove harmful substances; stimulate appetite and digestion; cleanse mucous membranes; strengthen the stomach, liver, gallbladder, and intestines	many plants, especially herbs and spices; also fennel, carrots, celery
Zinc	aids in combating stress; decreases the burden on the liver	fish, meat, cheese, grains

Power

Detoxify with a feast of vitamins

Week

FEELING BETTER THROUGH EATING, NOT FASTING

Would you like to lavish a little more attention on yourself and pay more attention to your health? Do you wish you could banish that weary feeling–not just in the spring– and perk up your metabolism? Treat your body to a week of detoxifying meals, and you're bound to feel better–without feeling deprived. Prepare and eat the recipes given for this one-week eating plan, and in no time you will start feeling and looking healthier. Of course, you can prepare any of the recipes anytime to give your health and well-being a kick.

THE ONE-WEEK DETOX PLAN

Following are suggestions for seven days' worth of meals. You can follow the plan as given, or mix and match the recipes if you wish. The best start to the day is a breakfast of whole-grain bread or whole-grain granola with sliced fruit, and low-fat yogurt or cottage cheese. If you get hungry, snack on raw fruit and vegetables. Use the tables on pages 186 and 187 to select the varieties that cleanse the body. For best results, it is

important to drink as much liquid as possible during your detoxifying Power Week; however, avoid beverages with large amounts of sugar and caffeine. Spring water, of course, is ideal.

AT WORK ALL DAY?

If you're too busy to prepare two meals a day, you can still reap the benefits of a detox plan. Prepare one of the recipes for the evening meal. To the office, bring some fresh fruit, vegetables, and yogurt for the midday meal. Use the tables on pages 186 and 187 to help you choose detoxifying produce.

THE WEEK'S MEALS

Monday

- Low-fat granola with fresh fruit, or whole-grain black bread; buttermilk
- Harlequin Vegetable Salad; whole wheat baguette
- Asparagus and Shrimp Risotto; fresh pineapple

Tuesday

- Whole-grain black bread; acidopholous milk
- Salad of Endive and Cress ❋ Quick Potato Curry
- Brown Rice and Celery Root Pancakes; fresh fruit

Wednesday

- Low-fat granola with fresh fruit, or whole-grain black bread; buttermilk
- Watercress Soup ❋ Asparagus and Herb Omelet
- Linguine with Artichoke Sauce; fresh pineapple

Thursday

- Whole-grain black bread; acidopholous milk
- Cornmeal Patties with Radish Salad; Fresh fruit
- Arugula and Apple Salad; sautéed boneless chicken breast

Friday

- Low-fat granola with fresh fruit, or whole-grain black bread; buttermilk
- Fruit and Asparagus Salad; whole-wheat baguette
- Salmon with Sorrel Sauce; new potatoes; fresh pineapple

Saturday

- Whole-grain black bread; acidopholous milk
- Vegetable and Yogurt Bake
- Julienned Zucchini with Red Pepper Sauce; whole-grain black bread;
Potato Cream Soup with Arugula

Sunday

- Fresh fruit salad; whole-wheat rolls; lean cold meats; one egg
- Chervil in Aspic with Mustard Sauce ❋ Stuffed Artichokes
- Asparagus Salad with Prosciutto; baguette; fresh pineapple

Asparagus

Salad with

and crunchy pine nuts

Prosciutto

Serves 2: 1 lb white or green asparagus • Salt to taste • 1/2 tsp sugar • 1 tsp butter • 2 tbs cider vinegar • White pepper to taste • 3 tbs vegetable oil • 4 thin slices prosciutto • 2 tbs pine nuts • Fresh basil leaves

Wash and trim the asparagus, and peel the lower third of the stalks. Bring a small amount of water to a boil in a saucepan with a little salt, the sugar, and butter. Place the asparagus in a steamer insert and lower it into the saucepan. Cover tightly and steam for 5-8 minutes, until the asparagus is tender-crisp.

In a bowl, mix together the cider vinegar, salt, and pepper; then, thoroughly beat in the oil with a whisk. Drain the asparagus well and cut into chunks. Toss the asparagus in the dressing. Arrange on plates with the prosciutto. Toast the pine nuts in a dry nonstick skillet until golden. Scatter the nuts over the asparagus, adding a few fresh basil leaves, for garnish.

PER PORTION: 358 calories • 17 g protein • 32 g fat • 7 g carbohydrates

Asparagus Salad with Watercress

fresh herbs add a refined touch

Serves 2:
1 lb asparagus
Salt to taste
1/2 tsp sugar
1 tsp butter
1/2 bunch watercress
1-2 tbs walnuts
1-2 tbs chopped mixed fresh herbs
1 tbs cider vinegar
White pepper to taste
1 tbs walnut oil
2 tbs vegetable oil

Wash and trim the asparagus, and peel the lower third of the stalks. Bring a small amount of water to a boil in a saucepan with a little salt, the sugar, and butter. Place the asparagus in a steamer insert and lower it into the pan. Cover tightly and steam for 5-8 minutes, until the asparagus is tender-crisp. Drain well and cut into chunks.

Wash the watercress well and shake dry. Sort it, removing any coarse stems. Roughly chop the walnuts.

To make the dressing, mix the herbs with the vinegar and season with salt and pepper. Thoroughly beat the two oils into the mixture with a whisk. Season to taste.

Toss the asparagus and watercress in the dressing. Arrange on plates and sprinkle with the walnuts.

Watercress

This peppery salad green (or herb) is full of good and healthy things. Just 5 oz supplies the entire daily requirement of vitamin C. It also contains iron, important in blood formation, and calcium. Watercress purifies the blood and encourages the flow of urine, making it an ideal ingredient in a detox plan.

PER PORTION:

251 calories

6 g protein

22 g fat

7 g carbohydrates

power

Dandelion Greens Salad
a stylish springtime salad
with Goat Cheese

Preheat the oven to 425°F. Peel and chop the onion and garlic and whisk them together with the vinegar, salt, and pepper. Thoroughly beat in the oil using a whisk.

Wash and sort the dandelion greens. Shake thoroughly dry and tear into bite-sized pieces. Toss the leaves in the dressing and arrange on plates.

Wash the cherry tomatoes, halve or quarter them, and add to the salad.

Cut the goat cheese into four rounds and lay on top of the bread slices. Place in an ovenproof dish and bake on the middle oven shelf until the cheese is hot, but not yet melted. Place the bread on the plates with the salad and serve immediately.

Serves 2:
1 small onion
1 small clove garlic
1-2 tbs wine vinegar
Salt to taste
White pepper to taste
3 tbs safflower oil
4 oz baby dandelion greens
2 oz small cherry tomatoes
1 small round goat cheese (2 oz)
4 baguette slices

Dandelion greens

Dandelion greens contain substances that stimulate the appetite and the digestion. Kidney activity is enhanced by dandelion greens, which therefore have a diuretic effect. A bitter constituent, *choline*, acts on liver function, and encourages the flow of bile. Dandelion is popular as a medicinal plant for treating gallbladder, liver, and kidney problems.

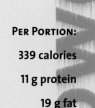

PER PORTION:

339 calories

11 g protein

19 g fat

9 g carbohydrates

power

Fennel and
with sautéed pork tenderloin
Grapefruit Salad

Peel the grapefruit with a very sharp knife, removing all of the bitter white pith. Cut down the sides of each membrane to release the fruit segments,

Serves 2:
1 pink grapefruit
1 bulb fennel
1 shallot
Salt to taste
Black pepper to taste
1 tbs cider vinegar
3 tbs canola oil
1/2 thin pork tenderloin
3 juniper berries
1 small handful arugula

collecting the juice in a bowl. Wash the fennel, trim it, and slice the bulb very finely. Chop the green fennel fronds and set aside.

Peel and finely chop the shallot. Whisk it together with the fennel fronds, salt, pepper, and vinegar in a bowl. Use a whisk to beat in 2 tbs of the oil, followed by the reserved grapefruit juice. Toss the fennel bulb and grapefruit segments in the dressing.

Rinse the pork with cold water and pat dry. Crush the juniper berries using a mortar and pestle, or chop with a large knife. Rub the pork with the crushed juniper berries, salt, and pepper. Heat the remaining 1 tbs oil in a large skillet over medium-high heat. Brown the meat on all sides, then reduce the heat to medium, and continue to cook for about 5 minutes, until done.

Wash the arugula, shake dry, and sort. Arrange on plates with the fennel and grapefruit salad. Cut the pork into thin slices and arrange on plates with the salad.

PER PORTION: 323 calories • 14 g protein • 23 g fat • 18 g carbohydrates

Purslane Salad

with slightly sweet apple dressing

with Green Beans

Serves 2:
3 oz green beans
Salt to taste
1 sprig fresh summer savory
or thyme
2 oz small white mushrooms
5 radishes
2-3 oz purslane
1 shallot
1 small clove garlic
Black pepper to taste
1 tbs cider vinegar
2 tsp unfiltered apple juice
(purchased or homemade)
2 tbs canola oil

Rinse and trim the beans, and halve if necessary. Bring a small quantity of salted water to a boil in a saucepan with the savory or thyme. Place the beans in a steamer insert, lower them into the saucepan, cover tightly, and steam for 10-15 minutes, until tender-crisp.

Meanwhile, rinse the mushrooms, or clean with a damp cloth. Slice them finely. Rinse and trim the radishes and cut into thin slices. Wash the purslane, shake dry, sort, and trim.

To make the dressing, peel and chop the shallot and the garlic. Stir them together with the salt, pepper, cider vinegar, and apple juice. Whisk in the oil thoroughly.

Drain the beans well and toss them in the dressing with the mushrooms, radishes, and purslane. Adjust the seasonings.

Purslane

This vegetable has green, fleshy leaves, which are rich in potassium and iron. Purslane helps flush out the system, and assists in blood formation. It also contains healthy omega-3 fatty acids.

PER PORTION:

123 calories

3 g protein

8 g fat

10 g carbohydrates

Raw Parsnip and Carrot Salad

a winter health boost

Toast the walnuts in a dry nonstick skillet until golden brown. Remove from the heat. Coarsely chop about 3 tbs of the walnuts and set aside.

Grind the remaining walnuts finely, and mix them with the cream, milk, oil, and vinegar, stirring until smooth. Season with coriander, salt, and pepper.

Select a small amount of the green parsnip tops, wash, shake dry, and chop finely. Stir the parsnip tops into the dressing.

Rinse and trim the parsnips and carrot. Slice them thinly or grate them. Arrange the vegetables on plates, drizzle with the dressing, garnish with the reserved chopped walnuts, and serve immediately.

Serves 2:

2 oz walnuts

1/4 cup heavy cream

1/4 cup milk

2 tsp safflower oil

1 tbs cider vinegar

Ground coriander to taste

Salt to taste

Black pepper to taste

5 oz parsnips (with tops)

1 small carrot

Parsnips

Parsnips are a good source of vitamins in the cold season of the year, when many other vegetables are unavailable. Just 7 oz of parsnips contain the daily requirement of vitamin C. In addition, parsnips stimulate the appetite and promote the flow of urine.

PER PORTION:

235 calories

5 g protein

17 g fat

18 g carbohydrates

power

Asparagus and
with crisp croutons
Avocado Salad

Cut away the crusts from the bread. Cut the bread into small dice. Heat the butter in a small saucepan until foaming. Fry the diced bread in the butter until golden brown on all sides. Cool.

Wash and trim the green onion and slice finely. Stir together with the apple juice, vinegar, salt, and pepper. Thoroughly beat in the two oils with a whisk. Rinse and trim the asparagus, and carefully peel the lower third of the stalks. Cut it diagonally into thin slices, and toss the slices in the dressing.

Wash the tomatoes, cut into wedges, and remove the tough portion next to the stalk. Peel the avocado, cut it in half, and remove the pit. Cut each half crosswise into slices. Sprinkle the slices with lemon juice.

Arrange the tomato wedges, avocado slices, and asparagus mixture on plates, sprinkling the tomatoes and avocado with some of the dressing. Scatter the croutons over the top.

Wash the lemon thyme and shake dry. Strip the leaves from the stalks and scatter over the salad. Serve immediately.

Serves 2:
1 slice whole-grain bread
1 tsp butter
1 small green onion
2 tsp unfiltered apple juice (purchased or homemade)
1 tbs cider vinegar
Salt to taste
White pepper to taste
1 tbs canola oil
1 tbs walnut oil
9 oz white or green asparagus
2 small, firm tomatoes
1 small avocado
1-2 tbs fresh lemon juice
1-2 sprigs fresh lemon thyme

PER PORTION: 243 calories • 4 g protein • 18 g fat • 17 g carbohydrates

Light
with yogurt dressing and pecans
Waldorf Salad

Serves 2: 1 super-fresh egg yolk • 2 tsp fresh lemon juice • 2-3 tbs canola oil • 1/4 cup plain yogurt • Salt to taste • Black pepper to taste • 2 stalks celery with leaves • 1 oz pecans • 1-2 tart apples

Stir together the egg yolk and lemon juice, then slowly whisk in the oil drop by drop. Stir in the yogurt. Season with salt and pepper. Rinse and trim the celery. Reserve the leaves and slice the stalks. Chop the nuts coarsely. Wash the apples, and cut them into 1/2-3/4-inch dice, removing the cores. Toss all the ingredients in the dressing, check the seasonings, and serve garnished with the reserved celery leaves.

PER PORTION: 325 calories • 5 g protein • 26 g fat • 20 g carbohydrates

Julienned Zucchini
a crunchy, vitamin-packed treat
with Red Pepper Sauce

Serves 2: 1 red bell pepper • Salt to taste • Black pepper to taste • Tabasco sauce to taste • 1 shallot • 1 small clove garlic • 1 tbs cider vinegar • 2 tbs olive oil • 4 oz zucchini

Rinse and trim the red pepper. Cut into fourths, and dice one piece finely. Puree the rest and push the puree through a sieve. Season the pepper puree with salt, pepper, and a few drops of Tabasco, and divide among serving plates. Peel and chop the shallot and the garlic, stir into the vinegar, season with salt and pepper, and beat in the oil with a whisk. Wash and trim the zucchini and cut into fine strips. Toss the strips in the dressing, then arrange on top of the red pepper sauce. Garnish with the diced red pepper.

PER PORTION: 101 calories • 2 g protein • 8 g fat • 5 g carbohydrates

Arugula Salad with
a cleansing salad with a taste of Italy
Two Cheeses

Toast the pine nuts in a dry nonstick skillet until golden brown. Set aside.

Trim and sort the arugula, wash it, and shake dry. Tear it into smaller pieces if necessary. Peel the carrot and grate it coarsely. Cut the fontina cheese into strips. Grate the Parmesan cheese.

To make the dressing, peel the shallots and dice very finely. Whisk together with the balsamic vinegar, salt, and pepper. Then, beat in the oil thoroughly with a whisk. Adjust the seasonings.

Toss the arugula, grated carrot, and fontina cheese in the dressing. Sprinkle the salad with the pine nuts and grated Parmesan.

Serves 2:

2 tbs pine nuts

3 oz arugula

1 small carrot

2 oz fontina cheese

1 oz piece Parmesan cheese

2 small shallots

2 tbs balsamic vinegar

Salt to taste

Black pepper to taste

1/4 cup olive oil

Arugula

Also called rocket or rucola, this well-loved salad green (or herb) is a relative of cabbage and mustard greens. Like them, it contains volatile oils and organic acids, whose effect on the appetite is stimulating . Arugula is also rich in vitamin C. It rids the body of excess fluid and should certainly be featured on the menu in any detox plan.

PER PORTION:

346 calories

13 g protein

32 g fat

6 g carbohydrates

power

Harlequin
with herbs and pumpkin seeds
Vegetable Salad

Cut the red pepper in half, trim away the stem and inner ribs, and remove the seeds. Wash it. Peel the kohlrabi, and trim and wash the radishes,

Serves 2:
1 small red bell pepper
1 small kohlrabi
1/2 bunch radishes
4 oz cucumber
1 small onion
1 small clove garlic
2 tbs pumpkin seeds
4 sprigs fresh Italian parsley
Handful of fresh chervil
4 sprigs fresh dill
1 sprig fresh tarragon
2 tbs cider vinegar
Salt to taste
Black pepper to taste
2 tbs safflower oil
1 tbs pumpkin seed oil

reserving a little of the green tops of both. Wash or peel the cucumber.

Cut the red pepper, kohlrabi, and cucumber into approximately 1/2-inch dice. Slice the radishes thinly. Mix the vegetables together.

Peel and finely chop the onion and garlic. Put them into a salad bowl. Chop the pumpkin seeds and add to the mixture in the salad bowl. Wash the herbs, along with the kohlrabi and radish tops, shake them dry, and chop. Add the herb mixture to the salad bowl.

Put the vinegar in a small bowl, and season generously with salt and pepper. Beat in the two oils with a whisk. Adjust the seasonings, then pour into the bowl with the vegetables and toss well. Let the salad stand for 30 minutes to blend the flavors.

PER PORTION: 219 calories • 7 g protein • 18 g fat • 9 g carbohydrates

power

Fruit and
with strawberries and melon
Asparagus Salad

Serves 2:

10 oz green asparagus
1 tsp butter
Salt to taste
Sugar to taste
1/4 ripe cantaloupe
3 oz fresh strawberries
1 tbs cider vinegar
1 tsp honey
White pepper to taste
3 tbs canola oil

Wash the asparagus, trim it, and carefully peel the lower third of the stalks. Bring a small amount of water to a boil in a saucepan with the butter and a little salt and sugar. Place the asparagus in a steamer insert and lower it into the pan. Cover securely and steam for 5-8 minutes, until the asparagus is tender-crisp.

Meanwhile, remove the seeds and fibers from the melon. Use a melon baller to scoop out little balls of the flesh. Wash and drain the strawberries, trim, and halve or quarter them.

In a salad bowl, whisk together the cider vinegar, honey, and a little salt and pepper. Thoroughly beat in the oil with a whisk. Drain the asparagus thoroughly and cut it into pieces about 1¼ inches long. Toss the asparagus in the dressing, together with the melon and strawberries. Serve immediately.

power

PER PORTION: 167 calories • 3 g protein • 13 g fat • 9 g carbohydrates

Sauerkraut Salad
cleansing and rich in vitamins
with Cress

In a salad bowl, thoroughly whisk together the cider vinegar, apple juice, and oil. Season with salt, pepper, and curry powder. With a knife, cut the sauerkraut into small pieces. Toss it in the dressing. Carefully peel the pineapple, removing the brown "eyes." Cut out the tough middle core and dice the flesh. Cut the ham into dice or strips.

Rinse the cress under cold water and shake dry. Trim the cress and put it in the bowl with the pineapple and ham, and toss well.

Season the salad generously, and arrange it on serving plates garnished by the nasturtium leaves and flowers.

Serves 2:
2 tsp cider vinegar
1 tbs unfiltered apple juice
(purchased or homemade)
2 tbs canola oil
Salt to taste
Black pepper to taste
1/4 tsp curry powder
5 oz sauerkraut (drained)
1/4 fresh pineapple
2 oz boiled ham
1/2 bunch peppercress
Small handful nasturtium
leaves and flowers

Sauerkraut

Sauerkraut, or fermented cabbage, contains lactic acid and fiber to stimulate digestion. Lactic acid also has a cleansing effect. Fresh, raw sauerkraut is the most beneficial to the intestinal flora and digestion, and to health in general. It contains up to 60 percent more vitamins than canned sauerkraut. Look for it in a high-quality delicatessen or specialty foods store.

PER PORTION:

203 calories

6 g protein

12 g fat

19 g carbohydrates

Arugula and
light, refreshing, and crisp
Apple Salad

Toast the pine nuts in a dry nonstick skillet until light golden brown. Set aside. Wash the apple thoroughly, quarter, and core it. Dice the apple and sprinkle it immediately with the lemon juice.

Trim and sort the arugula, wash it, and shake it thoroughly dry. Tear into smaller pieces if necessary. To make the dressing, whisk together the apple juice, red wine vinegar, salt, and pepper in a bowl. Then, thoroughly beat in the two oils with a whisk. Adjust the seasonings. Toss the arugula and diced apple in the dressing. Arrange the salad on plates and scatter the reserved pine nuts over the top. Grate the Parmesan over the salad before serving.

Serves 2:

2 tbs pine nuts

1 small red-skinned apple

1 tbs fresh lemon juice

3 oz arugula

1 tbs unfiltered apple juice (purchased or homemade)

2 tbs red wine vinegar

Salt to taste

Black pepper to taste

2 tbs olive oil

1 tbs pine kernel oil

1 oz Parmesan cheese

Alternatives to pine kernel oil

If you can't find pine kernel oil, or for a variation on the salad, other oils and nuts can be used instead. For example, use walnut oil and walnuts, hazelnut oil and hazelnuts, or almond oil and almonds. For a less intense flavor, dilute the nut oil with a neutral one.

PER PORTION:

245 calories

5 g protein

20 g fat

15 g carbohydrate

Fresh Herb Salad

with velvety Parmesan sauce

with Dry-Cured Beef

Serves 2:

3 oz mixed fresh herbs

2 oz dry-cured beef (such as

Swiss Bundnerfleisch)

1 egg

2 tbs canola oil

3 tbs dry white wine

2 tbs cider vinegar

2 oz Parmesan cheese, grated

3 tbs plain yogurt

Salt to taste

Black pepper to taste

Wash the herbs thoroughly and shake dry. Pick them over, and remove the tough stalks. Cut the dry-cured beef into strips and mix with the herbs.

Whisk the egg in a bowl with the oil, wine, and vinegar. Place the bowl over a saucepan of hot water and cook over medium heat, whisking constantly, until a light, creamy sauce is formed.

Remove the bowl from the pan of hot water, and stir the Parmesan into the sauce until melted. Cool the sauce a little, stir in the yogurt, and season with salt and pepper. Arrange the herb mixture on plates, drizzle the sauce over it, and serve immediately.

Herbs

Wild or cultivated, all herbs are full of health-giving properties. Fragrant and low in calories, they stimulate the appetite and digestion, and help cleanse the system. Try dandelion greens, watercress, sorrel, basil, Italian parsley, and chervil. Or, use dandelion greens or arugula alone.

PER PORTION:

265 calories

20 g protein

18 g fat

1 g carbohydrates

power

Radish and

raw food with a touch of elegance

Kohlrabi Carpaccio

Serves 2: 1/2 bunch radishes • 2 small kohlrabi • 1 tbs balsamic vinegar • 1 tbs unfiltered apple juice (purchased or homemade) • 1/4 tsp mustard • Salt to taste • Black pepper to taste • 2 tbs olive oil • 2 tsp pumpkin seed oil • 1 tbs pumpkin seeds

Wash and trim the radishes and kohlrabi. Peel the kohlrabi. Slice both vegetables thinly. Mix the vinegar, apple juice, mustard, salt, and pepper. Beat in the two oils. Arrange overlapping slices of kohlrabi in a circle on each plate. Arrange the radish slices inside the ring, circle in overlapping slices. Drizzle the dressing over the top and garnish with the pumpkin seeds.

PER PORTION: 154 calories • 3 g protein • 12 g fat • 11 g carbohydrates

Salad of Endive

a vitamin boost for chilly days

and Cress

Serves 2: 2 small oranges • 5 tbs plain yogurt • Salt to taste • White pepper to taste • Ground coriander to taste • 2 tbs grapeseed oil • 1-2 tbs ketchup • 8 oz Belgian endive • 1/2 bunch peppercress

Peel and segment the oranges, collecting the juice in a bowl. Mix the juice with the yogurt, salt, pepper, coriander, grapeseed oil, and ketchup. Wash and trim the endive, and cut into pieces. Rinse the cress under cold water, shake dry, and trim. Arrange the orange and endive on serving plates, drizzle with the dressing and scatter the cress over the top.

PER PORTION: 146 calories • 4 g protein • 6 g fat • 18 g carbohydrates

Watercress

tempting and cleansing

Soup

Wash the watercress and remove any very tough stems. Set aside a few leaves for garnish. Peel and finely dice the onion. Melt 1/2 tbs of the butter in a saucepan over medium heat and sauté the onion in it until transparent. Add the watercress and sauté briefly. Add the vegetable stock and simmer for a few minutes over low heat.

Puree the soup in a blender and return it to the saucepan. Stir in the cream and bring the soup back to the boiling point.

Place the egg yolk in a cup and stir in a little of the hot soup until smooth. Pour the mixture back into the pan with the soup, and stir well; do not allow the soup to boil at this stage. Season the soup with salt and a few drops of lemon juice.

Melt the remaining 1/2 tbs butter in a skillet. Cut the bread into dice and sauté it in the butter until browned on all sides and crisp Scatter the croutons over the soup before serving, and garnish with the reserved watercress leaves.

Serves 2:
1/2-1 bunch watercress
1 small onion
1 tbs butter
1 cup vegetable stock
1/2 cup heavy cream
1 egg yolk
Salt to taste
Lemon juice to taste
1-2 slices whole-grain bread

PER PORTION: 364 calories • 6 g protein • 23 g fat • 28 g carbohydrates

Potato Cream Soup
with crunchy almonds
with Arugula

Peel, wash, and dice the potatoes. Peel and dice the onion. Melt the butter in a saucepan over medium heat and sauté the onion in it until translucent. Add the diced potato and the stock, cover, and simmer for 10-15 minutes over low heat. Meanwhile, toast the almonds in a dry nonstick skillet until light golden brown. Remove from the heat. Wash the arugula and shake it dry. Remove any tough stems and cut the rest into strips.

Puree the potato soup in a blender. Return it to the saucepan and bring it back to the boiling point. Season with salt and pepper. Add the strips of arugula to the soup. Stir the cream into the soup. Garnish with the almonds before serving.

Serves 2:
10 oz potatoes
1 small onion
2 tsp butter
2 cups vegetable stock
2 tbs sliced almonds
1 small handful arugula
Salt to taste
White pepper to taste
5 tbs heavy cream

Soup with a plus

The potassium-rich potatoes and the aspartic acid-rich arugula, with its diuretic properties, both play a part in cleansing. The extra liquid from the soup is a bonus: it flushes out the kidneys.

PER PORTION:

299 calories

5 g protein

19g fat

26g carbohydrates

power

Creamy Lentil
with smoky bacon
Soup

Put the lentils and vegetable stock in a saucepan and bring to a boil.

Reduce the heat to low and simmer, covered, for about 40 minutes.

Cut the bacon into thin strips. Wash and trim the green onions, and cut them diagonally into small rings. Take a few lentils from the soup and set aside. Puree the remaining soup in a blender, and return it to the saucepan. Stir in the cream and reserved lentils and bring it back to the boiling point. Season with salt, pepper, and mustard; the soup should be boldly flavored.

Fry the bacon in a nonstick skillet until crisp. Add the green onions and toss them briefly in the bacon fat, without frying. Season with pepper. Pour the soup into bowls, sprinkle the bacon and green onions on top, and serve immediately.

Serves 2:

1/3 cup lentils

2 cups vegetable stock

1 oz bacon

1/2 bunch green onions

5 tbs heavy cream

Salt to taste

Black pepper to taste

1/2 tsp mild mustard

Lentils and mustard

Lentils are rich in fiber, which stimulates and protects the intestines, and prevents impurities from collecting. Mustard contains the glycoside *sinigrin* and the enzyme *myrosin*. Moisture causes them to react with each other, releasing volatile mustard oil, which has a cleansing, antiseptic effect on the body.

PER PORTION:

355 calories

14 g protein

21 g fat

25 g carbohydrates

Salmon and
light and luxurious
Asparagus Soup

Serves 2:
10 oz white or green asparagus
2 cups water
Salt to taste
Sugar to taste
2 tbs butter
4 oz fresh peas in the pod
(about 2 oz when shelled)
4 oz salmon fillet
1 tbs fresh lemon juice
1 tbs flour
1/4 cup crème fraîche

Wash and trim the asparagus. Peel it carefully, reserving the trimmings and peelings. Cut off the tips and set aside, covered. Cut up the asparagus stalks and place in a saucepan with 1/2 cup of the water, a pinch each of salt and sugar, and 1/2 tsp of the butter. Bring to a boil, cover, and cook for 15 minutes. Puree the cooked asparagus pieces with their cooking liquid.

Meanwhile, place the asparagus trimmings and peelings into another saucepan. Add the remaining 1 cup water, a pinch each of salt and sugar, and 1/2 tsp of the butter. Cover and simmer for 15 minutes. Strain and reserve the cooking liquid, discarding the solids.

Meanwhile, shell the peas. Wash the salmon and cut it into dice. Sprinkle it with the lemon juice.

Melt the remaining butter in a saucepan over medium-low heat. Stir in the flour and cook until the mixture turns golden brown. Pour in the strained asparagus cooking liquid and stir well; add the asparagus puree and crème fraîche.

Place the asparagus tips, peas, and salmon in the soup, and cook through for 2-3 minutes. Season the soup and serve immediately.

PER PORTION: 291 calories • 15 g protein • 21 g fat • 10 g carbohydrates

Chilled Cucumber

refreshment for hot summer days

Soup

Serves 2: 9 oz cucumber • 5 oz plain yogurt • 5 tbs crème fraîche • 1/2 cup buttermilk • 1 clove garlic • Salt to taste • Black pepper to taste • 1 tomato • 2 sprigs fresh dill

Peel the cucumber and grate it coarsely. Place it in a bowl and stir in the yogurt, crème fraîche, and buttermilk. Peel the garlic, mince it finely, and stir it into the soup. Season with salt and pepper. Cover and chill for 2 hours. Wash the tomato and dill. Dice the tomato finely. Select the delicate fronds of the dill and pull them away from the coarser stalks. Scatter the dill fronds and tomato onto the soup and serve.

PER PORTION: 240 calories • 6 g protein• 20 g fat • 9 g carbohydrates

Sauerkraut

with piquant arugula cream

Soup

Serves 2: 1 small onion • 1 small potato • 1 tbs butter • 5 oz sauerkraut (drained) • 2 cups vegetable stock • 2 oz arugula • 1/4 cup crème fraîche • Salt to taste • Black pepper to taste

Peel and dice the onion and potato. Melt the butter in a saucepan over medium heat. Add the onion and potato and sauté until the onion is translucent. Add the sauerkraut and vegetable stock, cover, and simmer for 10 minutes. Wash and sort the arugula and puree it in a blender with the crème fraîche. Season with salt and pepper. Puree the soup, return it the saucepan, and bring it to the boiling point. Serve topped with the arugula cream.

PER PORTION: 211 calories • 3 g protein• 16 g fat • 16 g carbohydrates

Frothy Chervil

smooth and cleansing

Soup

Peel the onion and potatoes, and dice them coarsely. Melt the butter in a saucepan over medium heat. Add the onion and potatoes and sauté until the onion is translucent. Add the stock, cover, and simmer for at least 20 minutes over low heat.

Rinse the chervil, sort thoroughly, and shake dry. Set aside a little chervil for garnish. Chop the rest, and stir it into the soup.

Puree the soup and return it to the saucepan. Stir in the crème fraîche and heat the soup to the boiling point. Season with salt, pepper, and a little coriander. Whisk the soup with a hand blender or whisk to a frothy consistency, and garnish with the reserved chervil before serving.

Serves 2:

1 small onion

4 oz potatoes

1 tbs butter

2 cups chicken or vegetable stock

Large handful fresh chervil

1/4 cup crème fraîche

Salt to taste

White pepper to taste

Ground coriander to taste

Chervil

This delicate spring herb stimulates the circulation, cleanses the blood, and encourages the flow of urine and perspiration, all beneficial in a detox plan. It also has volatile oils and bitter constituents, which promote digestion by stimulating the secretion of stomach juices.

PER PORTION:

171 calories

6 g protein

15 g fat

14 g carbohydrates

Chervil in Aspic with
layers of appeal
Mustard Sauce

Boil the egg for 10 minutes, until the yolk is cooked hard. Rinse the egg in cold water and peel it. Wash, sort, and dry the chervil. Set aside a few pieces of chervil for garnish, wrapped in a clean, damp cloth and kept in a cool place. Chop the remaining chervil a little finer, and mix it into the stock.

Serves 2:
1 egg
Handful of fresh chervil
1/2 cup vegetable stock
1 pkg powdered gelatin
Salt to taste
White pepper to taste
Tabasco sauce to taste
2-3 tbs cottage cheese
3-4 tbs milk
1 tsp mild mustard

Sprinkle the gelatin over the stock in a saucepan and let stand for about 5 minutes. Heat gently, stirring, until the gelatin is fully dissolved.

Season the stock with salt, pepper, and Tabasco; the mixture should be piquant. Pour a small amount of the stock mixture into two ramekins or cups. Chill in the refrigerator until set.

Cut the egg in half crosswise. As soon as the gelatinized stock in the molds has set, place one half of the egg on each, cut-side down. Pour the remaining stock over the egg, and place in the refrigerator until set.

In a bowl, mix together the cottage cheese, milk, and mustard, and season with salt and pepper. Place the molds momentarily in hot water to loosen them, then invert them onto serving plates. Spoon a little sauce alongside each. Garnish with the reserved chervil and serve.

power

PER PORTION: 125 calories • 9 g protein • 5 g fat • 12 g carbohydrates

Light Herb Mousse

with radish vinaigrette

Sprinkle the gelatin over a few tablespoons of water in a cup and let stand for 5 minutes. Warm the mixture by standing the cup in hot water; stir

Serves 2:
1 pkg powdered gelatin
1 bunch mixed fresh herbs, such as sorrel, flat-leaf parsley, dill, basil, and/or tarragon
5 tbs plain yogurt
Salt to taste
White pepper to taste
5 tbs heavy cream
5 radishes
2 tsp cider vinegar
2 tbs vegetable oil

occasionally, until the gelatin has dissolved.

Wash and pick over the herbs, and shake dry. Set aside some of the herbs for garnish; chop the rest of the herbs finely.

Mix the dissolved gelatin with the yogurt and herbs. Season generously with salt and pepper.

Whip the cream until stiff, and fold it into the herb mixture. Transfer it to a small ring mold or to two cups. Cover, and place in the refrigerator to set.

Just before serving, wash, trim, and coarsely grate the radishes. Mix them with the cider vinegar and a little salt and pepper. Thoroughly beat in the oil with a whisk. Adjust the seasonings.

Place the mold or cups momentarily into hot water to loosen the edges. Invert the mousse onto a serving platter or plates. Garnish with herbs and pass the vinaigrette at the table.

PER PORTION: 215 calories • 4 g protein • 20 g fat • 3 g carbohydrates

Asparagus and
succulent and quick to make
Herb Omelet

Serves 2: 9 oz green asparagus • Salt to taste • 2 tbs butter • 1 tsp sugar • 4 eggs • 2 tbs milk

• White pepper to taste • 2 tbs chopped fresh Italian parsley • 1-2 tbs chopped fresh chervil

Wash and trim the asparagus and steam it for 5-8 minutes over a little boiling salted water, with 1 tsp of the butter, and the sugar. In a bowl, whisk together the eggs, milk, salt, pepper, and herbs. Make two omelets one after the other in a nonstick skillet with the remaining butter. Drain the asparagus well, wrap in the omelets, and serve.

PER PORTION: 246 calories • 17 g protein • 17 g fat • 6 g carbohydrates

Brown Rice and
with herbed yogurt
Celery Root Pancakes

Serves 2: 1/2 cup brown rice • Salt to taste • 5 tbs plain yogurt • 1 tbs cream cheese • White pepper to taste • 2 tbs chopped fresh herbs • 1 tsp unfiltered apple juice • 5 oz celery root • 2 eggs • Oil for frying

Cook the rice in 1 cup water until just tender, but still slightly firm, about 30 minutes. Mix the yogurt, cream cheese, salt, pepper, herbs, and apple juice. Peel and coarsely grate the celery root. Drain the rice, cool slightly, and mix with the celery root and eggs. Season with salt and pepper. Heat a small amount of oil in a skillet over medium-high heat. Spoon out portions of the rice mixture to fry a succession of small pancakes. Serve with the herbed yogurt.

PER PORTION: 354 calories • 13 g protein • 18 g fat • 36 g carbohydrates

Artichokes with a
imaginative company food
Duo of Dips

Place a large amount of salted water in a large saucepan with a few lemon slices. Cut off the stems of the artichokes. Cut off the top third of the leaves. Place the artichokes in the water and boil over medium heat for 40 minutes. The artichokes are cooked when the leaves can be pulled away easily. Boil the egg for 10 minutes, until the yolk is cooked hard. Peel and rinse the egg and separate the yolk and the white. Pass the yolk through a fine sieve, and mix it with the cider vinegar, salt, and pepper. Beat in the oil gradually. Wash the sorrel, shake dry, and remove the tough stalks. Chop the leaves. Dice the egg white finely. Mix the sorrel, egg white, and sour cream into the egg mixture. Season to taste; the mixture should be piquant. Wash, trim, and grate the radishes. Stir together the cream cheese and milk, season with salt, pepper, and a little cardamom; then stir in the grated radishes. Lift the artichokes out of the water and drain them. Serve with the dips.

Serves 2:
Salt to taste
Lemon slices
2 artichokes (about 18 oz each)
1 egg
2 tsp cider vinegar
White pepper to taste
3-4 tbs olive oil
1/2 bunch fresh sorrel
1/4 cup sour cream
1/2 bunch radishes
2 oz cream cheese
4-5 tbs milk
Ground cardamom to taste

Eating artichokes

Pull away one leaf at a time, holding the tops between your fingers. Dip the fleshy base of the leaf in one of the dips, and eat it by drawing the leaf base through your teeth to skim off the flesh of the vegetable. When you have pulled away all the leaves, you will find the inedible, fibrous "choke" in the middle. Scoop it out and underneath you will find the delicious, succulent "heart" of the artichoke.

PER PORTION:
381 calories
13 g protein
32 g fat
11 g carbohydrates

Cornmeal Patties

good eating at home or the office

with Radish Salad

Serves 2:

1/2 cup vegetable stock
1/3 cup cornmeal (finely ground)
1 small carrot
1 small kohlrabi
1/2 egg
1/2-1 bunch fresh dill
Salt to taste
Black pepper to taste
2-3 tbs bread crumbs
3 tbs vegetable oil
3/4 bunch radishes
2 tbs plain yogurt
1 tbs cream cheese
1/8 tsp ground cumin

Bring the vegetable stock to a boil. Add the cornmeal and cook over very low heat for 10 minutes, keeping the saucepan tightly covered. Peel the carrot and kohlrabi, and grate finely. Add the vegetables to the cornmeal and cook together for another 5 minutes. Transfer to a bowl. Stir in the egg and let the mixture cool a little.

Wash the dill and shake dry. Discard the tough stalks and chop. Stir the dill into the cornmeal mixture. Season with salt and pepper. Add enough bread crumbs to create a mixture that holds together well. Divide the mixture and shape into 4 equal-sized patties. Heat the oil in a nonstick skillet over medium-high heat. Fry the patties in the oil for 10 minutes over very low heat, turning occasionally.

Meanwhile, wash the radishes, and coarsely grate them. Stir together the grated radishes, yogurt, and cream cheese. Season with salt, pepper, and cumin. Serve to accompany the patties.

PER PORTION: 337 calories • 10 g protein • 18 g fat • 33 g carbohydrates

Ham and
with crunchy vegetables
Herb Dip

Cut the ham into very small dice. Wash, dry, and sort the herbs. Pluck the leaves away from the tough stalks. Reserve a few leaves for garnish, and chop the rest. Rinse the lemon in hot water and dry it. Grate the zest and squeeze the juice.

Mix the ham, herbs, lemon zest, lemon juice to taste, almonds, and cottage cheese. Season the dip generously with salt and pepper.

Remove the outer leaves of the endive. Cut the endive in half, and make a wedge-shaped cut to remove the core. Separate into individual leaves. Wash and trim the remaining vegetables. Cut them into long strips, just wide enough to manage easily when eating.

Arrange all the vegetables on a large platter, accompanied by the dip. Garnish with the reserved herbs and serve.

Serves 2:

2 oz boiled ham

Handful of fresh herbs

1/2 lemon

3 tbs chopped almonds

1/2 cup cottage cheese

Salt to taste

Black pepper to taste

1 head Belgian endive

1/2 small bunch celery

1 small zucchini

1 carrot

1 small kohlrabi

1 small red bell pepper

PER PORTION: 229 calories • 17 g protein • 12 g fat • 12 g carbohydrates

Asparagus and
chic and simple
Shrimp Risotto

Wash the asparagus, peel the lower third, and cut it into 1 1/4-1 1/2-inch pieces. Cut off the asparagus tips, cover, and set aside. Wash and trim the green onions. Cut the green parts diagonally into fine rings. Chop the white parts finely.

Serves 2:

9 oz asparagus
1/2 bunch green onions
1 tbs butter
2 tsp olive oil
7 oz Arborio rice
1/2 cup dry white wine
2 cups vegetable stock
Salt to taste
White pepper to taste
4 oz peeled cooked shrimp
1 oz Parmesan cheese, freshly grated

Heat the butter and oil in a skillet over medium heat. Add the white onion pieces and sauté until translucent. Add the pieces of asparagus stem, followed by the rice. Sauté briefly and pour in the wine. Cook over low heat, stirring occasionally, until the rice has absorbed all the liquid. Add the vegetable stock about 1/3 cup at a time, and cook, stirring occasionally, allowing each addition to be absorbed before adding the next.

After 10 minutes, stir in the asparagus tips and the green pieces of green onion. Cook the rice until tender, but still slightly firm in the center; the mixture should remain creamy. Add the shrimp, mix, and heat through. Season the risotto with salt and pepper, and sprinkle with Parmesan before serving.

power

PER PORTION: 622 calories • 26 g protein • 12 g fat • 85 g carbohydrates

Stuffed
with mushroom and ham filling
Artichokes

Preheat the oven to 350°F. Bring a large amount of salted water to a boil in a large saucepan, and add the lemon juice or vinegar. Cut off the stems of the artichokes. Remove the outer leaves, and trim off the tops of any very pointed leaves. Boil the artichokes in the water for 40 minutes over medium heat. They are cooked when the leaves can be pulled away easily and the bottom of the artichoke feels soft when a small knife is inserted into it.

Serves 2:
Salt to taste
2 tbs lemon juice or vinegar
2 large globe artichokes
1 onion
5 oz small white mushrooms
1 clove garlic
2 tbs olive oil
2 oz boiled ham
1-2 sprigs each fresh thyme, rosemary, parsley, and basil
2 slices whole-grain bread
2 oz Swiss cheese, grated
Black pepper to taste

Peel the onion and chop finely. Clean, trim, and chop the mushrooms. Peel and finely mince the garlic. Heat the oil in a skillet over medium heat. Add the onion and sauté until translucent. Add the garlic and mushrooms, and sauté over low heat for 5 minutes. Dice the ham finely. Wash, dry, and chop the herbs. Stir the ham and herbs into the mushroom mixture, and remove from the heat.

Lift the artichokes out of the water, and drain them thoroughly upside down. Fold open the outer leaves and pull out the soft leaves from the middle. Remove the hairy, inedible "choke" with a spoon, and discard.

Cut the bread into small dice, add to the mushroom mixture, and stir in the cheese. Season with salt and pepper. Stuff the artichokes with the filling. Place the stuffed artichokes side by side in an ovenproof dish, and bake in the middle of the oven for 20 minutes, until hot.

PER PORTION: 366 calories • 22 g protein • 21 g fat • 21 g carbohydrates

Salmon with

delicious served with new potatoes

Sorrel Sauce

Wash and sort the sorrel. Set aside a few leaves and chop the rest. Peel and finely chop the shallot. Melt 1/2 tbs of the butter in a small saucepan over medium heat. Add the shallot and sauté until translucent. Sprinkle with the flour, and cook briefly, stirring. Stir in the stock. Add the chopped sorrel. Cover, and simmer over low heat for 5 minutes.

Rinse the salmon fillets in cold water and pat dry. Melt the remaining 1/2 tbs butter in a nonstick skillet until frothy. Cook the salmon over low heat for 3-5 minutes on each side.

Stir the crème fraîche into the sorrel sauce and season with salt, pepper, and a pinch of sugar. Cut the remaining sorrel leaves into fine strips. Arrange the salmon and sauce on plates, and scatter strips of sorrel on top before serving.

Serves 2:

2 oz fresh sorrel

1 shallot

1 tbs butter

1/2 tbs flour

1 cup salmon stock or other fish stock

2 salmon fillets (6 oz each)

2-3 tbs crème fraîche

Salt to taste

White pepper to taste

Sugar

Sorrel

This lemony herb is rich in iron, vitamin C, and bitter constituents. It stimulates the appetite, has a diuretic effect, and promotes blood formation and cleansing. It is also beneficial to the liver. However, sorrel should not be eaten in excessive quantities, because the oxalic acid it contains forms insoluble calcium salts, which can lead to kidney stones.

PER PORTION:

438 calories

36 g protein

35 g fat

5 g carbohydrates

power

Multicolored

Asian inspiration with hot spices and vitamins

Vegetable Curry

Serves 2:
1-2 red chiles
1 clove garlic
1/2 oz fresh ginger
1/4 cup coconut cream
(unsweetened)
6 tbs vegetable stock
2 tbs soy sauce
1 tbs curry paste
2 stalks celery
1 carrot
1/2 bunch green onions
3 oz broccoli
2 oz bean sprouts
2 tbs vegetable oil
2 sprigs fresh mint

Slit open the chiles and remove the seeds. Wash and chop the chiles. Peel and chop the garlic and ginger. In a saucepan, heat the coconut cream with the stock, soy sauce, and curry paste until heated through.

Wash and trim and/or peel the celery, carrot, green onions, and broccoli. Slice the celery, carrot, and green onions finely. Separate the broccoli into small florets. Rinse the bean sprouts and drain thoroughly.

Heat the oil in a wok or skillet over medium-high heat. Add the chile and stir-fry for 1 minute. Add the celery, carrot, green onions, and broccoli, and stir-fry for another 2-3 minutes. Add the bean sprouts and stir-fry for another 3 minutes.

Pour the coconut sauce into the wok, and cook all the ingredients together for 1-2 minutes. Just before serving, wash and dry the mint and cut the leaves into thin strips. Sprinkle the mint over the vegetables and serve immediately.

PER PORTION: 245 calories • 20 g protein • 20 g fat • 12 g carbohydrates

Simmered
with broccoli and sheep's milk cheese
Red Lentils

Serves 2: 9 oz broccoli • 1 small onion • 1 tbs olive oil • 1/2 cup red lentils • 1 cup vegetable stock • Salt to taste • Black pepper to taste • 1 tsp fresh thyme leaves • 4 oz sheep's milk cheese

Wash and trim the broccoli and separate it into florets. Peel the onion, dice it finely, and sauté it in the oil in a wide skillet until translucent. Add the broccoli, lentils, stock, salt, pepper, and thyme. Cook for 15 minutes, until the lentils are tender. Crumble the cheese, and add to the lentils. Cook together for another minute, until heated through.

PER PORTION: 364 calories • 25 g protein • 14 g fat • 33 g carbohydrates

Vegetable and
a meatless meal from the oven
Yogurt Bake

Serves 2: • 1 1/4 lb mixed vegetables • 3 eggs • 8 oz whole-milk yogurt • 1 tsp flour • 1 oz chopped almonds • Salt to taste • Black pepper to taste • 1/2 bunch fresh Italian parsley • 1/2 bunch peppercress

Preheat the oven to 400°F. Wash and trim the vegetables, and cut into bite-sized pieces. Boil them for 5 minutes in a small amount of water; drain well. Separate the egg yolks from the whites. Mix the yogurt, flour, chopped almonds, salt, pepper, chopped parsley, cress, and egg yolks. Beat the egg whites until stiff and fold them into the mixture. Place the vegetables in a baking dish and pour the yogurt mixture over the top. Bake in the middle of the oven for 20-25 minutes, until set.

PER PORTION: 380 calories • 22 g protein • 21 g fat • 24 g carbohydrates

Asparagus Gratin with
with Swiss cheese and almonds
Herb Cream

Preheat the oven to 400°F. Wash and trim the asparagus and peel the lower third of the stalks. Bring a small amount of water to a boil in a saucepan with the salt, sugar, and butter. Place the asparagus in a steamer insert and lower into the saucepan. Cook, covered, for 5-8 minutes, until tender-crisp.

Butter a shallow ovenproof dish. Wash the herbs and shake dry. Strip the leaves from the herb stalks and chop them finely. In a bowl, mix the herbs, sour cream, and eggs. Season with salt and pepper.

Drain the asparagus thoroughly and place it in the buttered baking dish. Pour the herb-cream mixture over the top. Sprinkle with the cheese and almonds, and bake in the middle of the oven for 30 minutes.

Serves 2:

1 lb asparagus
Salt to taste
Sugar to taste
1 tsp butter
2 sprigs fresh tarragon
2 sprigs fresh thyme
2 sprigs fresh lemon balm
or sorrel
1 cup sour cream
2 eggs
White pepper to taste
2 oz Swiss cheese, grated
2 tbs sliced almonds

PER PORTION: 483 calories • 20 g protein • 41 g fat • 9 g carbohydrates

Linguine with
stylish and cleansing
Artichoke Sauce

Place a large amount of water in a saucepan, and add the lemon juice or vinegar and a little salt. Cut off the stems of the artichokes. Cut off the top half of the leaves. Pull off or trim the remaining leaves, and peel around the hearts with a sharp knife. Scrape out the inedible, hairy "choke" with a spoon. Immediately place the trimmed artichoke hearts into the pan of water. Bring to a boil, then cook for about 10 minutes, until the hearts are tender. Lift out and drain the artichoke hearts, then cut into pieces.

Peel and chop the onion. Peel the garlic and cut into strips. Wash the herbs, shake dry, and roughly chop the leaves. In another saucepan, bring a generous amount of salted water to a boil (use at least 2 quarts). Add the pasta and cook until just tender, but still slightly firm to the bite (*al dente*).

In a medium skillet, heat the oil over medium-low heat. Add the onion and garlic and sauté until translucent. Add the artichoke hearts and herbs. Add the wine, season with salt and pepper, and simmer gently until heated through.

Drain the pasta well and add it to the other ingredients in the skillet; mix well. Sprinkle with the Parmesan before serving.

Serves 2:

2 tbs fresh lemon juice or wine vinegar

Salt to taste

2 large artichokes

1 medium red onion

2 small cloves garlic

2 sprigs each fresh thyme and marjoram

1 small sprig fresh rosemary

8 oz linguine or spaghetti

6 tbs olive oil

6 tbs rosé wine

Black pepper to taste

2 oz Parmesan cheese, freshly grated

PER PORTION: 763 calories • 27 g protein • 31 g fat • 88 g carbohydrates

Quick Potato

a spicy Indian-style cleanser

Curry

Serves 2:
14 oz boiling potatoes
1 tbs vegetable oil
2 small tomatoes
1/2 bunch green onions
1 clove garlic
1/2 oz fresh ginger
1/2-1 green chile
1/2 tsp garam masala
1/4 tsp flour
4 oz plain whole-milk yogurt
1 tbs fresh lemon juice
Salt to taste
Black pepper to taste
1-2 tsp black sesame seeds

Wash and peel the potatoes and cut into bite-sized chunks. Heat the oil in a large skillet. Fry the potatoes over medium heat for about 20 minutes, stirring and turning frequently, until tender.

Cut an X in the round ends of the tomatoes. Plunge them into boiling water for a few moments, then remove the peels with a pairing knife. Cut the tomato flesh into dice. Wash and trim the green onions. Slice them finely into rings, reserving a little of the green portions for garnish. Peel the garlic and ginger. Slit open, trim, and wash the chile. Chop the garlic, ginger, and chile, and add to the skillet with the potatoes, together with the green onions. Sauté the mixture briefly and stir in the garam masala.

In a bowl, blend the flour and yogurt until smooth. Stir into the potato mixture, then add the tomatoes. Cook over low heat for another 10 minutes.

Season the potato mixture with the lemon juice, salt, and pepper. Sprinkle with the green onion pieces and sesame seeds, and serve immediately.

power

PER PORTION: 205 calories • 6 g protein • 7 g fat • 30 g carbohydrates

Asparagus and
a fresh Asian-style combination
Chicken Stir-Fry

Serves 2: 1/2 bunch green onions • 2 oz shiitake mushrooms • 1 carrot • 14 oz asparagus • 7 oz boneless chicken breast • 1 tbs canola oil • 1 tbs soy sauce • 5 tbs dry white wine • Black pepper to taste

Wash, trim, and chop the onions, mushrooms, and carrot. Wash the asparagus, peel the lower third of the stalks, and cut into pieces. Cut the chicken into cubes. Heat the oil in a wok over medium-high heat, and stir-fry the asparagus and carrot for 3 minutes. Add the mushrooms and onions, and stir-fry for 2 minutes. Move the vegetables aside and stir-fry the chicken until browned on all sides. Add the soy sauce and wine, season, and stir-fry all ingredients for 3 minutes.

PER PORTION: 309 calories • 32 g protein • 6 g fat • 31 g carbohydrates

Tagliatelle with
a quick and delicious dish
Asparagus

Serves 2: 1 onion • 9 oz asparagus • Salt to taste • 7 oz spinach tagliatelle • 1 tbs butter • 1/2 cup vegetable stock • 4 oz cream cheese • White pepper to taste• Fresh chervil leaves

Peel and finely dice the onion. Wash, trim, and peel the asparagus. Slice it, leaving the tips whole. Cook the pasta in boiling salted water until just tender and drain. Meanwhile, sauté the onion and asparagus in the butter until the onion is translucent. Add the stock, cream cheese, salt, and pepper. Cover and cook for 10 minutes. Garnish with chervil and serve with the pasta.

PER PORTION: 551 calories • 18 g protein • 20 g fat • 77 g carbohydrates

Asparagus and
with stylish red rice
Chicken Ragout

Wash and trim and asparagus and peel the lower third of the stalks. In a saucepan, bring 1 cup of the water to a boil with some salt and the sugar. Place the asparagus in a steamer insert and lower it into the pan. Cover with a tight-fitting lid and steam for 5-8 minutes, until the asparagus is tender-crisp. Drain, reserving the cooking liquid. Cut the asparagus into 1 1/4-inch pieces.

Serves 2:
1 lb white or green asparagus
3 cups water
Salt to taste
1/4 tsp sugar
2/3 cup red rice or brown rice
7 oz boneless chicken breast
White pepper to taste
2 tbs butter
1 tbs flour
1 cup chicken stock
2 sprigs fresh chervil or Italian parsley

Meanwhile, bring the remaining 2 cups water to a boil in a saucepan. Add the rice, cover the pan tightly, and cook over low heat for 30-40 minutes, until the rice has absorbed all of the water. Meanwhile, rinse the chicken in cold water and pat dry. Cut it into 1-inch cubes and season with pepper.

Melt the butter in a saucepan over medium-high heat. Add the chicken and cook until golden brown on all sides; remove from the pan. Sprinkle the flour into the butter, stir, and cook until golden. Stir in the stock, blending it in well.

Pour in the asparagus cooking liquid, and cook over high heat, stirring, until the mixture becomes creamy. Wash the chervil or parsley, and chop or tear it into pieces. Stir it into the sauce, and add the asparagus and chicken. Return to a boil, season with salt and pepper, and serve with the rice.

power

PER PORTION: 494 calories • 34 g protein • 14 g fat • 65 g carbohydrates

Index

Credits

Published originally under the
titles Fatburner Rezepte:
Mit dererfolgreichen Glyx-Formel
biszu 7 Pfund in 7 Tagenweniger,
Beauty Food: Natürliche Schönheit für
Haut und Haar, Säure BasenBalance:
Topfit und gesund mit Leichtigkeit,
Entschlacken Mit Genuss: FürVitalität
und Wohlbefinden
©1999-2000 Gräfe und Unzer
VerlagGmbH, Munich

English translation copyright for the
US Edition ©2004 Silverback Books,Inc.

Authors: Marion Grillparzer,
Martina Kittler, Dagmar Von Cramm,
Angelika Ilies

Photographer: StockFood Eising,
Munich

ISBN: 1-59637-010-6

Printed in China

Caution

The techniques and recipes in this
book are to be used at the reader's
solediscretion and risk. Always consult
a doctor before beginning a new
eating plan.

Notes and Recipes

Notes and Recipes

Notes and Recipes